Lorraine Richardson is an experienced property solicitor and trainer who is a popular conference and CPD speaker. Lorraine is now freelance but when in practice she ran a branch office and was a partner and the COLP for her firm.

She also designs and delivers property and legal skills related courses and on-line materials including Conveyancing Quality Scheme training for the Law Society.

Lorraine has developed a skill for writing and delivering webinars and aims to produce work that is both interesting and accessible for the viewer. Lorraine is the major writer for the monthly update journal for practitioners, the '*Practical Lawyer*'.

Lorraine has set up her own company, Adapt Law Limited, and offers property related courses and webinars and a membership scheme for firms to access her webinars and personalised conveyancing training.

For more information go to www.adaptlaw.co.uk

A Practical Guide to Residential Freehold Conveyancing

A Practical Guide to Residential Freehold Conveyancing

Lorraine Richardson

M.A. (Cantab)

Law Brief Publishing

Published 2022 by Law Brief Publishing, an imprint of Law Brief Publishing Ltd
30 The Parks
Minehead
Somerset
TA24 8BT

www.lawbriefpublishing.com

Paperback: 978-1-914608-08-7

For Tiddy

PREFACE

I have worked in the conveyancing arena since I qualified in 1991 and have taught the subject for almost as long. I have been fortunate enough to write a number of conveyancing textbooks and course manuals over the years for organisations kind enough to offer the work to me. However, in so doing, I have always had to follow a syllabus and someone else's format. I have finally decided to write a book which focuses on the areas of conveyancing which, in my opinion, represent most risk or which those doing the work find most difficult (often these are one and the same).

In addition to teaching thousands of solicitors, conveyancers, paralegals and support staff over the years, I have also worked as a locum in a wide range of firms. This exposure to both the people doing conveyancing and the firms offering conveyancing services has given me an insight into the areas which are those doing the work of conveyancing find most difficult.

I sincerely hope that the people who read this book will find it a handy reference guide as to why many of the steps in the conveyancing process are taken.

It appears that the process of me writing a book involves self-imposed deadlines which I regularly miss, coupled with Tim's infectious enthusiasm and Garry's quiet patience. So, once again, my thanks go to Tim and Garry at Law Brief Publishing for giving me the opportunity to write this book; the second in the 'Conveyancing Companion' series.

And, once again, I also thank my family for letting me chase these flights of fancy. I would be nothing without their unerring support.

The law described in this book is up to date as at 30 March 2022.

Lorraine Richardson
March 2022

LEGAL NOTICE

Conveyancing is by its nature a risky business. Throughout this Practical Guide suggestions to assist conveyancers in managing some of these risks are made. However, risk cannot be eliminated, it can only be mitigated. It is the responsibility of those in practice to ensure that they comply with their legal and regulatory obligations. We are not attempting to cover every issue that a conveyancer might encounter in a residential freehold transaction. This Practical Guide discusses day-to-day challenges and issues for conveyancers and endeavours to provide suggestions to assist.

We have made every effort to ensure that the content of this Practical Guide is accurate. However, any outcomes or recommendations are just our opinion as to what steps you might wish to take in practice. The contents of this Practical Guide do not constitute legal advice and must not be relied upon as advice.

ABBREVIATIONS

Cilex – Chartered Institute of Legal Executives

CLC – Council for Licensed Conveyancers

CQS – Conveyancing Quality Scheme

Dreamvar – *P&P Property Ltd v Owen White & Catlin LLP and another and Dreamvar (UK) Ltd v Mishcon de Reya and another [2018] EWCA Civ 1082*

FCA – Financial Conduct Authority

HMLR – Her Majesty's Land Registry

HMRC – Her Majesty's Revenue & Customs

Lender's Handbook – UK Finance Mortgage Lender's Handbook for Conveyancers

LSAG Guidance – Legal Sector Affinity Group Anti-Money Laundering Guidance for the Legal Sector 2021

LPA 1925 – Law of Property Act 1925

LRA 1925 – Land Registration Act 1925

LRA 2002 – Land Registration Act 2002

LRR 2003 – Land Registration Rules 2003

MLRO – Money Laundering Reporting Officer

Protocol – Law Society Conveyancing Protocol

1989 Act – Law of Property (Miscellaneous Provisions) Act 1989

SRA – Solicitors Regulation Authority

TLATA 1996 – Trusts of Land and Appointment of Trustees Act 1996

RESOURCES

Throughout this Practical Guide, conveyancers are referred to source material for further detail or guidance. HMLR regularly reviews its procedures, accordingly, practitioners should ensure that they refer to the latest copy of any HMLR Practice Guide or document referred to.

The key source material is listed below and, where quoted, copyright is fully acknowledged.

HMLR website and Practice Guides

https://www.gov.uk/government/organisations/land-registry

Practice Guide 82: Electronic signatures accepted by HM Land Registry

Practice Guide 19: Notices, restrictions and the protection of third-party interests in the register

Practice Guide 57: Exempting documents from the general right to inspect and copy

Practice Guide 79: Local land charges

Practice Guide 81: Encouraging the use of digital technology in identity verification

HMLR forms

We refer to a number of HMLR forms in this Practical Guide – a link to all of them is here:

https://www.gov.uk/government/collections/hm-land-registry-forms

HMLR blog

https://hmlandregistry.blog.gov.uk/

Law Society Practice Notes

www.lawsociety.org.uk

The Law Society has issued the following practice notes of use to conveyancers and where are mentioned in this Practical Guide:

Property and Registration Fraud (26.06.2020)

https://www.lawsociety.org.uk/en/topics/property/property-and-registration-fraud#sub-menu-dy14

SRA

https://www.sra.org.uk

CLC

https://www.clc-uk.org/

CONTENTS

INTRODUCTION

Conveyancing is a process driven area of legal work. The use of property technology and digitisation has transformed the conveyancing landscape beyond recognition. We are consistently bombarded with 'prop tech' that, we are told, will be a 'game changer' for conveyancers. It is undoubtedly the case that harnessing technology to assist with the more mundane aspects of the conveyancing transaction has changed the work of the coalface conveyancer. However, has this innovation improved the process for the conveyancer or, most importantly, their client? Let's consider some questions:

Is conveyancing today a quicker process than it was in 1991? No.

Is conveyancing today a less stressful process than it was in 1991? No.

So why hasn't this exponential growth in the use of technology improved the conveyancing process for everyone working in it and the clients purchasing those services? There is no single answer to this complex question, of course, but here are some observations.

Some organisations have tried to distil conveyancing to a series of mechanistic, usually online, tasks to such an extent that they have forgotten that central to the process is people usually moving from one house to possibly their dream home. At its core, conveyancing is a people business. This requires the people carrying out conveyancing to have the appropriate skills. IT skills are a given. The ability to use a case management system properly and efficiently is also a given. But these skills can be taught. What is often missing is the ability to communicate effectively. We forget that behind death and divorce, conveyancing is probably the third most stressful reason for members of the public having to consult a lawyer. Remember that most people do not *want* to consult or pay for a lawyer; it is a necessity for them.

So how do we help those at the conveyancing frontline communicate effectively? They can have good telephone skills. They can have good typing skills and be able to email or send a pre-generated update. However, central to all of this is a basic understanding of the conveyancing process itself. It is simply not possible for someone at the frontline to communicate meaningfully if they do not know what stage the conveyancing process has reached, or the reason why a perceived delay might have occurred.

We must also add to this the fact that working in a legal office is different to many other office environments. Those in the conveyancing department will have to deal with a huge volume of communications received on any given day whether by telephone or email. But it is necessary for those working in the frontline to understand with whom they can communicate and what they can tell them. We might receive a call or email from the client, or a relative of theirs, an estate agent, a mortgage broker, even the client on the other side – but who are we entitled to talk to? It is necessary for anyone working in a conveyancing department to understand the professional conduct obligations imposed on firms carrying out conveyancing work which includes the all-important duty of confidentiality.

Therefore, at the heart of conveyancing, is the need to empathise with the client and to understand the conveyancing process itself. Many people working in a conveyancing department only work on a particular aspect of the transaction; often referred to as a 'silo' approach to work. A team member might only deal with file opening and client care matters, or preparing contract packages or work in the post completion team. There is no doubt that these people will gain an in-depth knowledge of their particular area of the process but this will result in team members not knowing what comes before their particular part of the process or after it.

Conveyancing is like a jigsaw puzzle. It is only once the last piece is in place that we see and understand the full picture. This Practical Guide aims to give those who only do part of the conveyancing process in their job or who are relatively new to the process the whole picture. It is hoped that it will also be helpful for those taking professional examinations such as the Solicitors Qualifying Examination, Cilex and Council for Licensed Conveyancers.

So, does this mean that an experienced conveyancer does not need to buy this Practical Guide? Not necessarily. Conveyancing work is fraught with risk and the management of that risk is a constant battle for those who work in and run conveyancing departments. 'Knowing what you don't know' is a key part of risk management. If a member of conveyancing staff is aware of a problem or a risk and is also aware that they cannot deal with it, they will be able to pass the file to a more experienced colleague which, in turn, will help the firm manage conveyancing risk more effectively.

We also cannot consider the conveyancing process without referring to some of the land law which provides the legal foundation upon which our procedure stands. In addition, throughout this Practical Guide, conveyancers will be prompted to consider practical issues and risks under the heading 'Practice Points'.

There will therefore be various themes which run through this Practical Guide as follows:

- Land law links
- Risks and how to mitigate them (including in outline, issues such as Money Laundering, cybercrime and professional conduct)
- Practice Points

This Practical Guide will focus on the tasks which paralegals and support staff are most likely to encounter and will consider:

- Client care matters
- AML checks and money laundering risks
- How to draft contract of sale
- Investigation of a freehold registered title
- Pre-contract searches
- Preparing for completion
- Post completion

We will consider the freehold conveyancing process in England and Wales involved in moving from one residential property to another.

It is also fair to point out what this Practical Guide will *not* cover which includes: leasehold transactions, planning matters and unregistered title.

There are some excellent, comprehensive conveyancing textbooks on the market and this Practical Guide does not attempt or intend to replace that reference material. The purpose of this Practical Guide is to provide in an accessible, easy to use format, a straightforward explanation of why many of the steps in the conveyancing process are taken.

We will not reproduce any of the standard conveyancing forms, for example the Law Society Protocol forms, but, where relevant, we will provide links for you to find them.

There are also a number of extremely useful resources on the HMLR website explaining how to carry out a number of standard registration tasks, such as using the portal, completing some of the forms and the new Digital Registration process. We will not repeat those processes but will direct you to the appropriate resources.

Every conveyancing firm will approach the work of conveyancing in a slightly different way. There are a number of case management systems on the market, a number of different providers of the standard conveyancing forms and each firm has its own policies, procedures and attitudes to risk. Anyone working in a conveyancing department should ensure that they understand their own firm's processes as they work through this Practical Guide. We will focus on what is considered to be best practice but readers must understand that their firm might have a different approach and if in doubt, should find out their firm's processes and requirements in any given part of the transaction.

Virtually every issue covered in this Practical Guide could form the subject of a book. This Practical Guide does not attempt to explain the underlying law and practice in relation to all issues covered – there are more detailed textbooks on the market that carry out this function. This Practical Guide attempts to outline *why* certain steps in the conveyancing process are taken and point out to conveyancers some of the risks and pitfalls involved. This Practical Guide is not a substitute for studying the subject in detail but, rather, is intended to be a handy reference guide for conveyancers at the coalface.

There are many excellent, experienced conveyancers who simply do not have the time to explain the conveyancing process to those who work with them. Many conveyancing support staff and paralegals understand what to do in terms of process but many do not understand *why* they are doing it. The central purpose of this Practical Guide is to explain to those staff why they are taking the steps in the conveyancing process. We will see that the risks in conveyancing are many and varied. These are highlighted throughout this Practical Guide but are also summarised in Chapter 10.

If we had to summarise one message in relation to conveyancing in this Practical Guide it would be: 'If in doubt, ask'.

The term 'conveyancer' is used to describe fee earners, whether qualified or not, who have conduct of conveyancing transactions.

The law is believed to be correct and up to date as at 30 March 2022.

CHAPTER ONE

CONVEYANCING, LAND LAW AND TRANSACTION OVERVIEW

This chapter will consider the fundamental question of 'what is conveyancing?' and will take a brief look at some underlying land law concepts. Land law is the legal framework upon which the practical process of conveyancing stands. We will then move on to look at an overview of a standard residential freehold conveyancing transaction. It is essential for a conveyancer to understand the conveyancing process in its entirety and, in particular, the significance of the two key stages, exchange of contracts and completion. We will refer to the overview throughout this Practical Guide.

Important terminology

Conveyancing and land law are littered with technical terms and concepts. You should always ensure that you understand the meaning of any such terms before you use them; if necessary, look them up.

Some of the most common terminology which you might come across is as follows:

> **Chattels** – this is the traditional term for what we would call fittings and describes movable, personal property for example, furniture or curtains. The distinguishing feature of chattels and fittings is that they are not fixed to the land and therefore do not pass with the land automatically when it is sold.

> **Contract for sale** – a contract for the sale of land must be in writing and the standard form of contract used for residential conveyancing in England and Wales is the Law Society contract which incorporates the Standard Conditions of Sale (Fifth edition – 2018 revision). You will see from the overview of the conveyancing transaction that the seller's conveyancer drafts the contract and this is the document which creates the legally

binding promise to sell and buy the property upon exchange of contracts (see Chapter 8). A valid contract simply needs to be signed by or on behalf of the parties to it – contrast this with the signing requirements for a deed (below).

Covenant – this describes a promise to do or not to do something. A 'restrictive covenant' is a promise *not* to do something; for example, 'not to use the property for any purpose other than a private dwellinghouse'. The distinguishing feature of a restrictive covenant is that it does not require any positive act to comply with it. This contrasts with a 'positive covenant' which *does* require steps to be taken to comply with it. For example, 'to keep the fence on the northern boundary of the property in good repair'. You can see that to keep the fence in good repair requires the payment of money. Covenants are also contained in leases, but we do not discuss leasehold covenants in this Practical Guide.. The law relating to covenants is complex. If certain conditions are met, it is possible for a restrictive covenant to 'run with the land'; this means that successive owners of the land taking the burden of the covenant can be sued for non-compliance. In the freehold context, the burden of a positive covenant does not pass to successive owners; we therefore have to find other ways of trying to enforce positive covenants. We will see that covenants affecting freehold land appear on the charges register of title (see Chapter 4).

Deed – title to land can only be transferred by deed (s52 LPA 1925) which is a special type of document that complies with certain statutory requirements. To be a valid deed the document must be:

- **in writing**
- **intended on the face of it to be a deed** (the document usually describes itself as a deed)
- **validly executed** (that is, signed). Each individual must sign the document in ink or other indelible medium. Each individual signature must be witnessed by someone who is physically present at the time the signatory signs the document. The witness must sign beneath the

signature of the party to the deed (with their signature, printed name and address). Note that one party to the deed cannot witness the signature of another party to the deed. The final requirement of valid execution is that the document is 'delivered as a deed' which means that the parties to the deed expressly or impliedly acknowledge by words or conduct their intention to be bound by the terms of the deed. The most common deeds in conveyancing are the transfer (TR1) and mortgage deed.

Contrast these signing requirements with a contract (above).

Easement – this is the right of one landowner over the land of another. The land which benefits from a right is called the 'dominant tenement' and the land over which the right is exercised is called the 'servient tenement'. The right must benefit the land in some way, rather than merely be a right which is of only personal benefit to the landowner. The list of the rights which are capable of being an easement is always increasing but the most common easements which you will come across in freehold conveyancing are a right-of-way (for example, the right to cross the land of another to gain access to the public highway), a right of support for adjoining buildings or a right to use pipes and cables which cross the land of another. Importantly, for an easement to be valid, the land taking the benefit and the land taking the burden must be owned by different people. It is not possible for someone to have a right-of-way over their own land, for example. An easement must be created by deed (see above); commonly this will either be in a transfer of part (TP1) on a plot sale on a new build development or in a separate deed of easement.

Mortgage – in conveyancing terms, a mortgage is an agreement between a lender and a borrower to secure a loan. The lender is called the 'mortgagee' and the borrower is called the 'mortgagor'. The lender will take a legal charge over the title of the land owned by the borrower as security for the loan. Importantly, the lender does not become the legal owner of the land; they simply have the benefit of the legal charge which is we will see, appears on the charges register of a title (see Chapter 4). In a typical residential conveyancing transaction, the lender will provide a significant sum of money on completion to assist the buyer to purchase the property. This is called the 'capital' sum. A typical residential mortgage runs for 25 years over which time the buyer agrees to repay the capital sum plus interest on the outstanding debt. As we will see, the lender will set out the terms of the borrowing in a mortgage offer (see Chapter 7). A mortgage is another legal interest in land that can only be created by deed (see above) – in this case, the mortgage deed. If the buyer does not keep up the mortgage repayments, the lender has the right to take court action against the borrower to recover the property (that is, repossess the property) and to sell the property to recover the amount owing.

What is conveyancing?

In its purest form, 'conveyancing' describes the transfer of the legal title in a piece of land from the legal owner to another party. Traditionally, the main role of the lawyer was to establish that the seller had good title to the land and ensure that the legal title was transferred by deed. As we know, the role of the conveyancer now extends well beyond this process and includes many other aspects including complying with money laundering requirements, carrying out searches, advising on any mortgage financing, to name but a few.

You might see the seller referred to as a 'vendor' and the buyer referred to as a 'purchaser' in older documents, but we now stick to the terms 'seller' and 'buyer' as this is the terminology referred to in the standard contract of sale (see Chapter 6).

Land law links

We cannot talk about conveying title to land without a basic understanding of the legal concepts of land and title to it. The LPA 1925 defines 'land' which includes:

- the surface of the land and the ground beneath the land
- buildings on the land

- mines and minerals beneath the land (though things such as coal and oil are governed by statute)
- trees and plants growing on the land
- the air above the surface of the land (to such height as is necessary for the ordinary use and enjoyment of the land)
- fixtures
- rights which benefit the land such as a right of way over neighbouring land

All of the above pass from the seller to the buyer when a piece of land is sold.

A fixture is attached to the land and forms part of the land when it is sold. Contrast this with 'fittings' which are items that are not fixed to the land and therefore do not form part of the land. As we will see, this distinction is important when the seller's conveyancer drafts the contract and asks the seller to complete the Fittings and Contents Form.

Freehold and leasehold

This Practical Guide deals with freehold conveyancing but we do need to have an outline understanding of the difference between freehold and leasehold. When we talk about conveyancing, we tend to say that someone 'owns' their land. Strictly, this is not correct. All land in England and Wales is owned by the Crown.

Land law links

The development of land law has taken place over many hundreds of years and what a land 'owner' in fact has is an 'estate' in land. An estate is, essentially, the right to use the land and under s1 LPA 1925 there are two legal estates:

1. **the freehold estate** – the holder of the freehold is entitled to use the land indefinitely
2. **the leasehold estate** – the holder of the leasehold is entitled to use the land for a fixed, maximum duration which is set out in a document called a 'lease'. A leaseholder might have the right to use the land for many hundreds of years but even so, the nature

of the leasehold estate is that there is an ascertainable date upon which the lease will end

For the sake of convenience, we will refer to a seller as being the 'owner' of the land which they are selling but remember that the legal position is as above.

Commonhold is another form of land ownership which was introduced in 2002. It is essentially a hybrid form of ownership between freehold and leasehold and was introduced to try to alleviate a number of the perceived deficiencies in the leasehold form of ownership. It has not proved popular in practice and we will not mention it further.

Legal and beneficial interest in land

You should have a basic understanding of co-ownership, which is the situation which arises when two or more people acquire an interest in land together.

English land law has developed a clear distinction between the holder of the legal title and the behind-the-scenes, beneficial interest. The formal legal title to land is owned separately from the beneficial ownership of it. The holder of the legal title and the beneficial ownership may be the same parties but this will not necessarily always be the case. The law recognises that whilst the holder of the legal title has the right to possess or use the property and can sell or transfer it, they may not have the right to the economic benefit of the property that is, the sale proceeds when a property is sold.

We will see that the holder of the legal title appears on the proprietorship register (see Chapter 4). An important feature of English land law is that the holder of the beneficial interest is said to be 'behind-the-scenes' meaning that the party entitled to the sale proceeds when a property is sold will not appear on the register of title and a buyer is not entitled to enquire as to their identity.

This division between the legal title and the beneficial interest has developed over time due to the application of the principles of equity, that is, fairness. The law recognises that if someone has contributed money towards the purchase of a property, they should be entitled to recover that money when the property is sold, even if they do not appear on the legal title. It is for this reason that the beneficial interest is often also referred to as the 'equitable interest' in a property.

Land law links

Note that the legal title can only be held by a maximum of 4 people who are of full age (over 18) with mental capacity (s34(2) LPA 1925). There is no limit on the number of people who can have a beneficial interest.

There are two methods of co-ownership which must be explained to buyers when more than one of them are purchasing a property together. Most conveyancing firms will have a standard letter or report detailing this information. These are:

Joint tenants – parties who as joint tenants do not have a separate 'share' in the property; they are all equally entitled to the property. The principle of 'survivorship' applies to this form of co-ownership and provides that on the death of one co-owner, their interest in the property passes to the surviving co-owners automatically. This means that owners who hold as joint tenants cannot dispose of their property will by or the intestacy rules if they have not made a will.

Note that the legal estate can only be held as joint tenants (s 36(2) LPA 1925).

The beneficial interest can be held as joint tenants or using the second form of co-ownership:

Tenants in common – parties who hold as tenants in do have a separate 'share' in the property. The doctrine of survivorship does not apply to the tenancy in common. Thus, on the death of a tenant in common, their share in the property will pass in accordance with their will or the intestacy rules if they have not made a will. The risk for a buyer is that there might be someone behind the scenes *other than the legal owner* who has a claim on the slae proceeds where there is a tenancy in common.

Co-owners who hold as tenants in common can agree to hold the beneficial interest in the property in whatever shares they wish. If parties are contributing to the purchase price in unequal shares, their conveyancer will usually advise that the beneficial interest is held as tenants in common. This would enable the party contributing the greater share to recover this amount when the property is sold. The conveyancer will advise parties holding as tenants-in-common to reflect their agreement in a separate document called a 'declaration of trust' and because there is no survivorship, they will advise the parties to each prepare a will. Preparation of these documents usually involves additional legal fees. Note that whilst the conveyancer will give the parties the advice, the clients do not have to take that advice.

In general, as we have seen, a buyer is not concerned with who owns the beneficial interest in the property and, indeed, is not entitled to this information. Note that a conveyancer acting for a buyer should not request a copy of a declaration of trust or a will as these are not documents of title. A buyer must be able to safely purchase the property even if there are behind-the-scenes beneficial interests and this is achieved by the legal mechanism called 'overreaching'.

Overreaching – this is a very important land law principle that is relevant in everyday conveyancing practice. When land is held *by or for* more than one person, a 'trust of land' arises automatically (s1 TLATA 1996). This is the case whether or not the parties who acquire the interest in the land are aware of it. If they are properly advised when they purchased, their legal adviser should inform them about the legal and beneficial interest but even if they are unaware, a trust of land arises automatically. We have seen that if there is more than one owner of the legal estate, it must be held as a joint tenancy. The parties who hold the legal estate are called the 'trustees'.

We have also seen the idea that the equitable interests under the trust are hidden behind the legal ownership. This is known as the principle of the 'curtain'. A buyer will not be concerned as to the beneficial interests behind the 'curtain', only that the purchase price is paid to those who are legally entitled to deal with the legal title. The beneficial interest in the property can be held as joint tenants or tenants in common and in general, a buyer is not concerned with who owns the equitable interests or the basis upon which they are held.

The risk for the buyer is that the holder of the legal estate (in the registered system this is the registered proprietor – see Chapter 4) might not be entitled to the purchase money. The holder of the legal estate might be holding the legal title on trust for a behind-the-scenes beneficiary who is entitled to all of the sale proceeds. However, the law has developed a mechanism to protect a buyer in this situation, provided that the correct formalities are followed.

The reason that a buyer need not be concerned about the behind-the-scenes beneficial interest is due to the doctrine of *overreaching*. Provided that the buyer pays the purchase money to the trustees of the legal estate being at least two in number or a trust corporation, the interest of the behind the scenes beneficiaries is converted from an interest in the land to an interest in the sale proceeds in the hands of the trustees.

A trust corporation is a legal entity which carries out the administration of trusts and estates which can hold assets in England and Wales as well as abroad. Traditionally they were set up by banks and private client law firms.

Practice Points

It is unlikely that in general residential conveyancing, you will come across the legal estate of a property being held by a trust corporation very often. However, we do need to consider when a buyer should pay the purchase money to two trustees to ensure that any behind-the-scenes beneficial interest transfers from the land to the sale proceeds. This is of huge significance to a buyer. If the purchase money is not paid to two trustees, this means that any behind-the-scenes beneficial interest continues to bind the land. A behind-the-scenes beneficiary, of whom the buyer would have no detailed knowledge, may have a claim against the buyer of the land once their purchase completes.

> *How do we know if there is a behind-the-scenes beneficial interest which should concern buyer?*

In the registered land system, you need to look at the proprietorship register.

If there are between two and four people named on the proprietorship register (the holders of the legal estate), and there is no Form A restriction on the proprietorship register, this means that the registered proprietors also hold the beneficial interest as joint tenants. Remember that if a joint tenant dies, their interest in the property passes automatically to their surviving co-owners.

However, if there are between two and four people named on the proprietorship register and there is a Form A restriction on the proprietorship register, this means that the registered proprietors hold the beneficial interest as tenants in common.

The wording that you are looking out for on the proprietorship register is as follows:

RESTRICTION: No disposition by a sole proprietor of the registered estate (except a trust corporation) under which capital money arises is to be registered unless authorised by an order of the court.

(See HMLR PG19).

See Chapter 4 for more information regarding the registers of title.

So overreaching is the conversion of an equitable interest in land to an interest in the sale proceeds provided that a buyer pays the purchase money to a trust corporation or two or more trustees of the legal estate. HMLR is only interested in recording the ownership of the legal estate, not the beneficial interests. As far as possible, specific references to trusts are kept off the register of title. The registered proprietors are the owners of the legal estate. We do not necessarily know whether they, or any other persons, are the owners of the equitable interests. A person dealing with the registered proprietors can assume that they have unlimited powers to dispose of the property unless there is a restriction on the register limiting their powers. The presence of a Form A restriction on the proprietorship register denotes a behind-the-scenes beneficial interest and alerts a buyer to the fact that the purchase money must be paid to two trustees.

If a buyer is purchasing from two or more registered proprietors, no further action needs to be taken because as we have seen, there are two trustees of the legal estate already in place who can give a valid receipt for the purchase money to ensure that overreaching takes place.

However, if a buyer is purchasing from a single registered proprietor and there is a Form A restriction on the proprietorship register, this tells you that there is a behind-the-scenes beneficial interest. It will therefore be necessary for the seller to agree to appoint a second trustee in the transfer document to ensure that overreaching takes place.

Remember that the effect of overreaching is to transfer the interest of any behind-the-scenes beneficiary from the land to the sale proceeds. This means that anyone who has a claim against the sale proceeds will be able to pursue the trustees who gave the receipt but, crucially for the buyer, they will not be able to pursue the buyer after their purchase has completed.

Let's just recap:

> **One registered proprietor and no Form A restriction** – a buyer can buy from the sole registered proprietor
>
> **Two registered proprietors and a Form A restriction** – a buyer can buy from the two registered proprietors. Although the restriction denotes a behind-the-scenes beneficial interest, we already have the two trustees in place to overreach.
>
> **One registered proprietor and a Form A restriction** – the buyer must be careful! A buyer must ensure that a second trustee is appointed to overreach the beneficial interest.

As ever, this is a complex area of land law and conveyancing and this is only an outline explanation to ensure that you can recognise when a second trustee should be appointed. If you do not have experience of dealing with this aspect, it is vital to ensure that a qualified professional amends the contract and approves the transfer document as required to ensure that there are no problems after completion. Once again, the ability of a conveyancer to recognise this issue is an important risk management tool.

Overview of the conveyancing transaction

Below is an outline of a standard conveyancing transaction. Part of the challenge of understanding conveyancing is knowing what stage the transaction has reached. Accordingly, we will refer to the overview as we work through this Practical Guide.

SELLER	BUYER
MARKETING STAGE OF THE TRANSACTION	
Markets property with an estate agent Obtains Energy Performance Certificate Sale agreed Conveyancer is instructed	Views property Makes offer to buy property Agrees price via estate agent Conveyancer is instructed
PRE-EXCHANGE STAGE OF THE TRANSACTION	
Conveyancer takes instructions from client: • Identification / due diligence / AML • Client care letter	Conveyancer takes instructions from client: • Identification / due diligence / AML • Client care letter
Obtain seller's title Ask seller to complete Protocol forms	Obtain money on account for searches
Draft sale contract	
Send contract package to buyer's conveyancer: • Contract in duplicate • Seller's title • Protocol forms • Any guarantees, planning permissions etc	Submit pre-contract searches, typically: • Local search • Drainage search • Environmental search Are any specialist searches required?
	Investigate title Receive and review search results
	Raise pre-contract enquiries

Liaise with seller and reply to pre-contract enquiries	
	Resolve how the buyer will finance the purchase: • Cash and/or • Mortgage
	Report to client on the title, search results and replies to enquiries
	Obtain funds from the buyer for the deposit paid on exchange of contracts, typically 10% of the purchase price
Seller and buyer agree suitable moving date (completion date) and inform their conveyancer	

EXCHANGE STAGE OF THE TRANSACTION

This is the point at which the transaction becomes legally binding. The buyer pays 10% of the purchase price as the deposit on exchange and the completion date (the moving date) is agreed and inserted into the contract.

EXCHANGE	EXCHANGE

PRE-COMPLETION (OR POST EXCHANGE) STAGE OF THE TRANSACTION

Often there are two weeks between exchange of contracts and completion

Obtain redemption figure on seller's mortgage (if any)	
	Draft transfer
Approve transfer Seller to sign transfer	

Prepare completion statement	Prepare completion statement Obtain funds to complete: • Request any cash due from buyer and/or • Submit Certificate of Title to lender
	Submit pre- completion searches: • Bankruptcy search (if buyer is getting a mortgage) • HMLR Official search with priority (OS1) **RISK!** It is essential to ensure that the 30-working day OS1 priority period expiry is diarised
Fill in Completion Information and Undertakings Form (2019) **RISK!** Who is authorised to give the undertaking to redeem the seller's mortgage/s?	Check Completion Information and Undertakings Form (2019) to ensure that the seller's conveyancer has given an undertaking to pay off all of the seller's mortgages from the sale proceeds

COMPLETION STAGE OF THE TRANSACTION

This is the moving date that was agreed in the contract on exchange

This is the date that the buyer's conveyancer sends the balance of the purchase money in return for the title to the property which passes from the seller to the buyer in the transfer document

Completion date	Completion date
	Send completion money to the seller's conveyancer via bank transfer **RISK!** What steps are taken to check where the completion money is being sent to?

Confirm receipt of completion money Inform buyer's conveyancer Inform seller client Contact estate agent to confirm that keys can be 'released' to the buyer	

POST COMPLETION STAGE OF THE TRANSACTION

The seller and the buyer have moved and are generally no longer interested in their conveyancer!

This is the stage of the transaction where some important work has to be done by the conveyancers acting for the seller and the buyer

Send transfer and any other documents to buyer's conveyancer	Pay Stamp Duty Land Tax (SDLT) (if any) within 14 days of completion
Redeem mortgage/s if any	
Pay estate agent's account, if approved by the seller	
Send evidence of removal of mortgage/s if any to buyer's conveyancer and obtain release from undertaking given on completion	Register title (and mortgage, if any) within priority period of OS1 search **RISK!** It is vital for the buyer's conveyancer to submit the HMLR in time
	Check completed registration for accuracy
Close file	Close file

CHAPTER TWO

REGULATION, PROFESSIONAL CONDUCT AND CLIENT CARE

Conveyancing involves significant risk for a homeowner. It is usually the biggest financial transaction that people enter into and it is essential to ensure that good title to a property is obtained. Accordingly, most people will take professional legal advice when they sell or buy a property (it is, technically, possible for someone to act for themselves although in practice this will be very rare). Law firms offering legal services are subject to professional obligations. This Chapter will consider in outline the regulation of conveyancing firms which will lead us to some fundamental professional conduct issues: confidentiality, undertakings and conflicts of interest. We will then look at client care issues.

Stage of the conveyancing process

SELLER	BUYER
MARKETING STAGE OF THE TRANSACTION	
Markets property with an estate agent Obtains Energy Performance Certificate Sale agreed Conveyancer is instructed	Views property Makes offer to buy property Agrees price via estate agent Conveyancer is instructed
PRE-EXCHANGE STAGE OF THE TRANSACTION	
Conveyancer takes instructions from client: • Identification / due diligence / AML • Client care letter	Conveyancer takes instructions from client: • Identification / due diligence / AML • Client care letter

Regulation

Law firms offering legal services to the public are subject to regulation by professional bodies. This is to ensure that appropriate ethical standards are maintained when acting for clients to protect them. Part of this protection is a requirement that regulated law firms have professional indemnity insurance in place which is designed to recompense a client who suffers loss due to the actions of a law firm. Another part of the protection is that regulated law firms and qualified lawyers working in them are subject to professional conduct rules.

The two main regulators for law firms which carry out conveyancing work are:

> **the Solicitors Regulation Authority (SRA)** – this is the organisation that regulates solicitors in England and Wales. The rules that solicitors and firms must comply with are known as the Code of Conduct which includes the Solicitors Accounts Rules. The Code and Accounts Rules are contained in the SRA Handbook which can be found online.
>
> Link: https://www.sra.org.uk/solicitors/standards-regulations/code-conduct-solicitors/
>
> **the Council for Licensed Conveyancers (CLC)** – this is an organisation that regulates specialist conveyancing and probate lawyers. Conveyancing firms will either be regulated by the SRA or the CLC. Lawyers who qualify via the CLC are known as licensed conveyancers and they must comply with the CLC Handbook which sets out regulatory principles and responsibilities. This includes a Code of Conduct and Accounts Code.
>
> Link: https://www.clc-uk.org/handbook/the-handbook/

A solicitor is a professional qualification which allows the person to carry out any type of legal work although most solicitors tend to specialise in a particular practice area, such as conveyancing. A person with a specialist conveyancing qualification is a licensed conveyancer.

Conduct

Rules of professional conduct are a set of standards with which regulated professionals must comply. A failure to meet the appropriate standards could lead to the regulated professional having their right to practice removed. Both solicitors and licensed conveyancers must meet the standards of their respective regulator and, importantly, must ensure that the people working with them in the conveyancing department do not breach these standards.

Working in any office environment can involve the use of computers and case management systems, the need to communicate effectively (whether by letter, email or telephone) and the ability to interact with colleagues and clients. However, working in a legal environment also carries with it additional responsibilities some of which are particularly relevant to conveyancing. We will highlight three of the main areas of conduct which affect those working in a conveyancing department but note that this is only an outline and in practice, dealing with these issues can be complex.

Undertakings

An undertaking means *'a statement, given orally or in writing, whether or not it includes the word "undertake" or "undertaking", to someone who reasonably places reliance on it, that you or a third party will do something or cause something to be done, or refrain from doing something'* (SRA Glossary).

In essence, an undertaking is a professionally binding promise which the party receiving it is entitled to rely on. There are a number of problems with undertakings which means that it is easy to give an undertaking accidentally. For example:

- an undertaking can be given orally. This means that you could give an undertaking on the telephone. Best practice demands that the terms of an undertaking are agreed between both parties and written down, but it is not a requirement that an undertaking is in writing

- an undertaking can be given by anyone in a law firm, it does not have to be given by a qualified professional. This means that a member of the conveyancing team could give an undertaking which binds the firm or the solicitor or licensed conveyancer for whom they work

- the word 'undertaking' does not need to be used for a statement to be construed as such. Thus, you could accidentally give an undertaking without knowing

Anyone giving an undertaking should ensure that they are able to comply with the undertaking at the time that they give it. For example:

'I will send you the transfer signed by my client' is achievable if at the time the undertaking is given, the person making the promise holds the transfer duly signed by their client. However, if the client is not coming in until the following day, or the transfer is still in the post, it is not possible to comply with this undertaking at the time it is given. Therefore, the undertaking should be: 'I will send you the transfer signed by my client [as soon as my client has signed it] or [as soon as it is received by me]'.

Undertakings are important in the conveyancing process. For example, if a conveyancing firm wishes to obtain their client's unregistered title deeds from a lender, the firm will give an undertaking to the lender that upon receipt of the deeds, the firm will not release the title deeds to anyone until the mortgage is redeemed.

We will also see in Chapter 8 the importance of the undertaking to redeem a seller's mortgage out of the sale proceeds on completion of a sale.

Best practice demands that undertakings are only given and signed by qualified professionals or someone with sufficient training.

Confidentiality

Rule 6.3 of the SRA's Code of Conduct for solicitors states that solicitors must *keep the affairs of current and former clients confidential unless disclosure is required or permitted by law or the client consents.*

Rule 3.6 of the CLC's Code of Conduct imposes the following obligation on conveyancers *Clients' affairs are treated confidentially (except as required or permitted by law or with the Client's consent).*

These obligations are broadly the same and mean that solicitors and licensed conveyancers are obliged to keep client matters confidential and, crucially, to ensure that everyone working in the firm does so.

Conflicts of interest

A conflict of interest is a situation where '*your separate duties to act in the best interests of two or more clients in relation to the same or a related matters conflict.*' (SRA Glossary).

Rule 6.1 of the SRA's Code of Conduct for solicitors states that solicitors must not act if their own interests conflict with those of a client, or there is a significant risk of such a conflict arising. So, in a conveyancing context for example, a solicitor should not act for a buyer if that buyer is purchasing a house owned by the solicitor.

Rule 6.2 of the SRA's Code of Conduct for solicitors states that a solicitor must not act if the interests of two or more clients conflict, or there is a significant risk of such conflict arising. There are a couple of exceptions to this rule but they do not apply to conveyancing.

Note that the SRA's rules provide that there does not have to be an *actual* conflict-of-interest, the *significant risk* of a conflict arising is enough for the solicitor to decline to act. If a conflict-of-interest arises during a transaction, the solicitor must cease continuing to act for both clients and must send them elsewhere. You can see how inconvenient and difficult this would be for clients during a transaction. Accordingly, it is important for solicitors and the people working with them to be alive to the possibility of conflict-of-interest and to try to avoid them before they arise. Thus, if we think that there might be a significant risk of a conflict-of-interest arising between two or more clients, we should not act in the first place.

The CLC has a separate Conflicts of Interest Code. A licensed conveyancer must not accept instructions from a person nor continue to act for a client whose interests conflict directly with those of the licensed conveyancer, the firm or another client. Note that the CLC and the SRA diverge in their attitude to conveyancing firms acting for the seller and the buyer in the same transaction – see below.

Practice Points

The key to all conduct issues is awareness. You should always think about conduct issues and, before taking any steps such as sending a document or telling someone that you will do something, take time out to ask a qualified professional. This is an important part of risk management which we have mentioned before – being aware enough to avoid taking a step is important. For example:

Confidentiality

Has someone telephoned you or emailed you asking for information about your client's transaction? If they have, but you are not sure who they are, do not reply to the email or give the information requested. Remember that even telling someone that you are instructed by a particular client could be a breach of your firm's duty of confidentiality to your client. So, a statement as simple as 'Yes, we are instructed by Miss Richardson regarding her purchase of 32 Avenue Road, Reading' could cause difficulty. If you are in any doubt as to whether you can deal with a party or give information, you should always check with your client first. Simply contact your client and seek their instructions. In terms of confidentiality, once the genie is out of the bottle, it cannot be put back.

Undertakings

Have you promised to send a signed document to the firm on the other side of the transaction? Have you promised to do something or ensure that something is done? If you have and the other party relies on that promise, your firm could be in breach of undertaking if you do not carry out that promise. As a general rule, try to avoid confirming that you will send documents or money unless you have checked with a qualified professional first or are absolutely sure that this is something that you can do.

Try to confirm any statements made on the telephone with a follow-up email and if in doubt, make it clear to the other party that you are not giving an undertaking to carry out the particular task. We will see in Chapter 8 that the conveyancing process is heavily reliant on professional undertakings and nowhere is this riskier for a conveyancing firm than when agreeing to redeem (that is, pay off) the seller's mortgage on a sale. This also links to the Completion Information and Undertakings form which is sent by the seller's conveyancer to the buyer's conveyancer just before completion.

Conflicts of interest

A good way to think about conflicts of interest is to consider whether advice to more than one client on the same transaction would be different. If this is the case, this would give rise to a significant risk of a conflict-of-interest and the conveyancer should decline to act or cease acting if the file is already open.

This is a complex area and generally, someone who is unqualified should not be suggesting to a client or any party in a conveyancing transaction that a conflict-of-interest has arisen. This is because the consequences are significant in that the firm must decline to continue acting for both parties if a conflict-of-interest arises. However, an important risk management tool for all conveyancing departments is the frontline conveyancing staff being aware of the possibility of conflict-of-interest and notifying a qualified professional accordingly.

It can be easier to think about conflicts-of-interest in a practical context. There are a number of situations in relation to conveyancing where a conflict between two or more clients could arise.

Acting for two people selling the property that they own – generally no conflict-of-interest arises in this situation because both clients want the same thing that is, to sell the property.

However, we need to be careful. For example, if your firm is acting for a married couple who are getting a divorce, this could be a problem if they cannot agree on issues such as the sale price or how the sale proceeds should be split between them.

Acting for two people who are buying a property – generally no conflict-of-interest arises in this situation because both clients want the same thing that is, to buy the property.

However, as you have seen above, if two people contribute to the purchase price of a property in unequal shares, your firm is likely to advise them to hold the beneficial interest as tenants in common. If the buyers cannot agree on this advice, a conflict-of-interest could arise.

Acting for seller and buyer in the same transaction – this is the classic 'conveyancing conflict' scenario. What we are talking about is a situation where, for example, Heather Smith is selling her house, 14 Hill Rise, Oxford and has agreed to sell it to James Miller for £140,000 and both Heather and James want to instruct the same conveyancing firm to act for them.

This is the situation where the view of the SRA and CLC differ.

A previous version of the SRA's Code of Conduct contained specific requirements which, if met, allowed the same firm to act for the seller and buyer in the same conveyancing transaction, subject to the overarching duty to act in the best interests of both clients. However, there are no such exceptions in the current Code and whilst the SRA does not say anything specific about acting for seller and buyer in the same transaction, their general position is that SRA regulated law firms should not be doing this is as a matter of course.

The CLC's position is different in that their Conflicts of Interest Code does allow the same conveyancing firm to act for the seller and the buyer in the same conveyancing transaction provided that:

- the seller and buyer are represented by different licensed conveyancers in the firm conducting themselves as if they were in separate firms; and
- before instructions are accepted, each client is informed in writing that the firm has been asked to act for the other party in the same transaction and the relevant issues and risks have been explained each client; and
- each client has provided informed written consent confirming that they agree to the firm acting for the other party

The above requirements are subject to an overriding requirement that the firm does not act or continue to act where the ability to give independent advice is restricted. The firm has a duty at all times to act in the best interests of each client.

Many conveyancing firms have internal policies and procedures which must be met relating to conflicts generally and the possibility of acting for the seller and the buyer in the same conveyancing transaction. It is important for people working in conveyancing firms to understand the regulatory framework and their own firm's procedures in this regard.

In all cases where you recognise the possibility of a risk of a conflict-of-interest, you should take a note of any conversation and inform a qualified professional immediately.

At the time a conveyancing file is opened, many conveyancing firms (whether SRA or CLC regulated) will carry out what they describe as a 'conflict check'. There is often a box to tick on a file checklist confirming that this has been done. Often, this is no more than a member of the accounts or administration team simply checking at the time the file is opened that the firm has not acted for the party on the other side. Whilst this is a helpful initial procedure to try to manage the risk of a firm avoiding conflict or breach of confidentiality, it does not remove the obligation on the conveyancer to be constantly vigilant to the possibility of a conflict of interest arising during a transaction. As with most conduct issues, these are not 'one off' matters but are part of a continuing duty to monitor the transaction from beginning to end.

We will consider other possible conflicts-of-interest which might arise in conveyancing later in this Practical Guide.

The 'client care' letter

Part of the regulatory function of the SRA and the CLC is to ensure that regulated organisations carry out their work to appropriate professional standards and an important element of this is that clients have a clear understanding of the work which will be carried out and the cost of that work at the beginning of a transaction. The contract between a firm and client is called the 'retainer'.

Rule 8 of the SRA's Code of Conduct for Solicitors requires that the solicitor identifies who they are acting for in relation to any matter and provides certain information to a client including at the time of engagement:

- the client's right to complain about the service and charges
- how a complaint can be made and to whom and
- any right to complain to the Legal Ombudsman

If a firm does not resolve a client's complaint within 8 weeks, they can complain to the Legal Ombudsman. The Ombudsman investigates complaints from members of the public about the service they have received from a legal service provider. The providers include solicitors and licensed conveyancers. This means that complaints about SRA and CLC regulated firms are dealt with by the Legal Ombudsman but note that a client must have exhausted a firm's internal complaints process before pursuing the matter via the Legal Ombudsman.

The SRA Code goes on to provide that complaints must be dealt with by the firm *promptly, fairly and free of charge*. The client must be given information in a way that they can understand and the client must receive the best possible information about how their matter will be priced. Importantly clients must be told about the likely overall cost and any other costs incurred at the time of engagement and as the matter progresses. Clients must also be told how the firm is regulated.

At beginning of any retainer, a firm will want to inform a prospective client about the work that will be carried out, the costs and the firm's terms and conditions. The SRA Code of Conduct does not prescribe that this information is given to a client in writing although the vast majority of firms will provide it in written format in a letter which is often called the 'client care letter'. An SRA checklist suggests that an effective client care letter is written in plain English and includes the following:

- a clear explanation of the agreed work, next steps and confirmation of what is and is not included in the work

- a concise and easy to understand breakdown of costs and explanation of any potential additional costs
- clear information on the likely timescales for the agreed work
- a clear explanation of the action required from the client and where they can obtain further information if needed
- details of a named contact in the firm and how to get in touch if the client has further questions

CLC regulated firms are subject to similar obligations regarding upfront information such as costs, work and complaints procedures in its Estimates and Terms of Engagement Code.

Practice Points

Many law firms have standard client care letters and terms of engagement for conveyancing which are sent to a prospective client at the beginning of the retainer. This is often the type of work which those joining a conveyancing department will do. Whilst it seems like a straightforward administration, it must be understood that the information contained in the client care letter is a regulatory requirement and underpins the contractual relationship between the firm and the client. Many firms will ask a client to sign and return a copy of the client care letter and/or terms of engagement as evidence of their acceptance of those terms. Some firms will send this information in the post. Others might use a case management system or app and send it electronically.

Transparency Rules

Most SRA and CLC regulated law firms must, since December 2018, comply with the Transparency Rules. The general purpose of the Rules is to assist potential clients to make informed decisions about legal services, including the cost. Amongst other things, the rules require law firms to prominently display price information on their website in a clear and understandable format. It must be clear whether VAT is chargeable and the basis of a firm's charging structure must be set out. If a firm uses an online quote generator, it must produce a quote for legal services without requiring any additional contact, for example someone calling to discuss the quote. The rules also require typical timescales and key stages to be indicated together with the experience and qualifications for all individuals who carry out work within the areas specified under the Rules. Conveyancing is just one of the areas of legal work covered by the Transparency Rules. If a firm does not have a website, the information should be provided in an alternative format.

Legal fees

It can be seen that a client must understand the likely level of costs that they are going to incur at the beginning of their conveyancing transaction. These outgoings must be broken down so that the client is clear as to:

> **The firm's legal fees** – often referred to as the firm's 'costs'. This is the amount that the firm will charge for carrying out the legal work. Every firm will calculate the costs slightly differently. Some firms may charge less for a sale transaction than a purchase. Others might offer a fixed fee conveyancing service meaning that the client will pay the same amount for the work carried out by the firm irrespective of how long the job takes or how complex the matter becomes. Some firms will charge for their work on an hourly basis (although this is relatively rare in conveyancing). Other firms may specify the cost of the legal work based on the price of the property in question but might reserve the right to increase the costs if the matter becomes more complicated. In this case, it is essential that the client is informed in advance of any potential costs increase.

> **VAT** – Value Added Tax (VAT) is a tax that is charged on most goods and services supplied by VAT registered businesses in the UK. A law firm's legal fees will be subject to VAT at the rate of 20%. It is important for a firm to indicate whether a not VAT is payable in relation to its legal fees. If this is not made clear, the legal fees will be deemed to include VAT.

> **Disbursements** – this is a term which is generally only encountered in a legal context. A disbursement is a payment made by a solicitor (or licensed conveyancer) to a third-party which is claimed back from the client. In essence, disbursements are any outgoings made in the course of a transaction which are not the firm's legal fees and VAT. It is generally very

straightforward to be specific as to the amount of disbursements which a client may have to pay in a conveyancing transaction, for example, the cost of obtaining official copies of the seller's title on a sale. There will be more disbursements on a purchase including pre-contract searches (see Chapter 7), SDLT and HMLR fees (see Chapter 8). Some disbursements are also subject to VAT which must be separately itemised.

Practice Points

'Disbursement' is a 'legalistic' word which many clients will not immediately understand. In the interests of transparency and clarity, firms could use a more straightforward term such as 'outgoings'.

It is worth noting that one of the most common complaints by clients about the providers of legal services is in relation to costs and the amount that a client has spent. A client will often indicate that the firm has charged more than they expected. Clarity on costs should start with the Transparency Rules on the firm's website. When the specifics of a client transaction are known, in particular the sale and purchase price of the property in question, the firm should be able to indicate with reasonable certainty and clarity the amount of the legal fees, VAT and disbursements (outgoings) that the client will incur in relation to that transaction. If the firm needs to increase its legal fees because the matter has become more complicated, it must notify the client in advance of any increase in legal fees and not simply present the client with a much higher bill at the conclusion of the transaction.

Note that most law firms will open a separate file for a sale transaction and a purchase transaction for the same client. This is to ensure that the documentation in relation to each transaction does not become muddled and the legal fees, VAT and disbursements (outgoings) are clear for each file. As you will see in Chapter 3, the firm will keep a separate accounts ledger for each file. This ledger will generally be electronic and will be monitored and maintained by personnel in the firm's accounts department.

If the same client has a sale transaction and a purchase transaction, these are usually 'related' transactions. This means that the client will need to sell the property that they are currently living in before or on the same day as the property that they are buying. It is essential that the conveyancer does not make any assumptions in this regard. If the client wants to move from one house to another on the same day, it is the job of their conveyancer to 'synchronise' the transactions.

Law Society

The Law Society is an organisation which represents solicitors in England and Wales. However, the Law Society has an important part to play in relation to conveyancing work because all conveyancers, whether solicitors or licensed conveyancers, will use the Law Society's standard conveyancing forms and will adopt the Conveyancing Protocol.

The Law Society Conveyancing Protocol is a statement of best practice to be adopted in relation to conveyancing transactions where there is the sale and purchase of a home for an owner occupier.

The Protocol is not used for new build transactions. The Law Society makes the point that it should not be used as a checklist and a solicitor has an overarching duty to act in the best interests of each client and those interests take priority over any steps set out in the Protocol.

The conveyancing transaction is broken down into a series of stages and the Protocol sets out the steps which the seller and buyer should be taking for their respective clients at the various stages of the transaction. The Protocol is a very helpful guide to the conveyancing transaction and you should read it.

Link: https://www.lawsociety.org.uk/en/topics/property/conveyancing-protocol

The Law Society also offers an accreditation scheme to try to ensure that accredited firms meet appropriate quality standard for residential conveyancing work. This is the Conveyancing Quality Scheme (CQS) and SRA regulated firms which carry out residential conveyancing can choose to apply for accreditation. Once the CQS accreditation is achieved, firms must ensure that all people carrying out conveyancing work undertake mandatory training and the firm must demonstrate compliance with the Protocol. This means that CLC regulated practices are not part of the CQS scheme and are not obliged to follow the

Protocol or use the standard conveyancing forms but, generally, will do so.

Law Society Conveyancing Forms

The Law Society introduced the 'Transaction' scheme and forms a number of years ago in an attempt to streamline the conveyancing process. The forms have been updated a number of times since they were originally introduced and are generally available to conveyancing firms through third-party software and forms suppliers. The forms are now almost universally adopted in standard residential conveyancing transactions. There are various forms, including the contract mentioned in Chapter 1, but the ones which will most commonly be encountered in a freehold residential conveyancing transaction are as follows:

Property Information Form (4th edition 2020 – second revision) – This form is completed by the seller and forms part of the contract package (see Chapter 6). It is designed to give the prospective buyer practical information about the property on issues including: boundary ownership and maintenance, whether there have been any disputes, planning matters, who lives at the property being sold, guarantees and warranties, whether the property has flooded and the services enjoyed by the property (for example, gas, electricity, foul drainage and water).

Fittings and Contents Form (3rd edition) (2013) – this form is completed by the seller and forms part of the contract package (see Chapter 6). It contains a list of items found in a typical residential property and the seller will indicate on the form which items are being left at the property on completion and which are being removed. We have already seen that items which count as fixtures form part of the land and are included when a property is sold and items which are merely fittings do not. The purpose of the Fittings and Contents Form is to avoid disputes between sellers and buyers as to what items are to be left at the property on completion.

The **Completion Information and Undertakings form** (3rd edition) is also one of the standard Protocol forms. We will consider this form in Chapter 8 when we look at pre-completion procedures.

Most people working in a conveyancing department will be familiar with the forms but if you are not, please follow the link below and look at the forms mentioned above.

Link: https://www.lawsociety.org.uk/en/topics/property/transaction-forms

Practice Points

Many people working in a conveyancing department will know how to access the Protocol forms and will send them to their seller client to complete at the beginning of a sale transaction. However, a key part of developing as a conveyancer and avoiding risks is to understand what the forms contain and why they are important. We will return to this theme as we work through this Practical Guide.

CHAPTER THREE

DUE DILIGENCE
AND MONEY

We saw in Chapter 1 that originally, the work of the property lawyer was primarily to ensure that the seller had good title to the land in question and that the buyer acquired that title in return for the purchase money. However, in recent years, the conveyancing landscape has changed enormously and nowhere is this more so than in relation to money and the financing of a purchase. This Chapter will briefly consider the Accounts Rules and will move on to look at anti-money laundering and due diligence requirements which includes the steps required to identify the client at the beginning of the transaction. We will briefly look at other types of fraud that conveyancers might encounter and the importance of identifying the 'red flags'.

Stage of the conveyancing process

SELLER	BUYER
MARKETING STAGE OF THE TRANSACTION	
Markets property with an estate agent Obtains Energy Performance Certificate Sale agreed Conveyancer is instructed	Views property Makes offer to buy property Agrees price via estate agent Conveyancer is instructed
PRE-EXCHANGE STAGE OF THE TRANSACTION	
Conveyancer takes instructions from client: • Identification / due diligence / AML • Client care letter	Conveyancer takes instructions from client: • Identification / due diligence / AML • Client care letter

Accounts Rules

We have seen that a key function of the regulation of solicitors and licensed conveyancers is protection of the public and nowhere is this more important than in relation to client money. Conveyancing firms can deal with many millions of pounds on a daily basis and it is vital for the integrity of the conveyancing process that members of the public and lenders can be sure that their money is protected.

SRA regulated law firms must comply with the Accounts Rules and firms must have systems and controls in place to ensure compliance with the rules. CLC regulated firms must comply with the CLC's Accounts Code. Both sets of rules are somewhat different but both have similar underlying principles.

The first is that money belonging to clients must be kept separate from money belonging to the firm or business. In a conveyancing context, client money includes money paid by a buyer towards their property purchase (whether the 10% deposit required on exchange or the balance required for completion) and mortgage advances paid by lenders. Money belonging to the firm or business can include money which partners have invested in the firm and money paid to the firm in payment of a bill rendered for the legal work carried out. Both sets of rules require the regulated firms to keep a 'client account' into which client money is paid. They must also keep a separate account for money belonging to the business which is usually called the 'business account' or 'office account'.

The second similar principle between the two sets of Accounts Rules is that client money and business money must never be mixed. It is also essential that client account is never permitted to become overdrawn. Regulated firms are obliged to maintain detailed accounts records and must produce an accountant's report.

Most conveyancing firms will have an accounts department which deals with the day-to-day running of client account and business/office account and those working in conveyancing departments must understand the procedures adopted by their firm in this regard.

Practice Points

A point of particular significance for conveyancing departments is that client money must be cleared through the banking system before it can be used. The reason for this is that it is a breach of the Accounts Rules to allow money belonging to one client to be inadvertently used for the purposes of another. For example, Brian Jones gives his conveyancer a cheque for £20,000 which is to be used for the 10% deposit for his house purchase. Usually, a cheque will take 5 days to clear through the banking system. If Brian's conveyancer exchanges contracts only 2 days after his cheque has been paid in and pays the deposit to the buyer's conveyancer that day, Brian's cheque will not have cleared at the time the money is used. If Brian's cheque fails to clear ('bounces') on day 3, his conveyancing firm will be in breach of the Accounts Rules because they have effectively used other client's money to fund his £20,000 deposit.

This is a very important rule and applies even if the sums of money are relatively small. Accordingly, you should always ensure that any money paid in by your client has cleared before you use it, perhaps on a purchase to pay for pre-contract search fees (see Chapter 7) or a deposit on exchange of contracts (see Chapter 8). Most conveyancing firms will maintain an electronic ledger of client transactions which you can check before paying out any money. If in doubt, ask someone in your accounts department!

We will see that most conveyancing firms will ask a buyer client for money on account of pre-contract searches.

Anti-Money Laundering (AML)

The law and procedures relating to AML is lengthy and complex. There are significant obligations placed on law firms and lawyers and the sanctions can be serious if something goes wrong. The main money laundering offences are contained in the Proceeds of Crime Act 2020 (as amended by the Criminal Finances Act 2017). An individual found to have committed an offence could be fined and/or imprisoned for a maximum of 14 years.

Many organisations are covered by the AML requirements including banks and a number of professional organisations. Conveyancing firms are at the forefront because they receive significant sums of money direct from clients. The challenge for firms is to try to avoid 'dirty money' being paid into client account.

'Money laundering is generally defined as the process by which the proceeds of crime, and the true ownership of those proceeds, are changed so that the proceeds appear to come from a legitimate source' (Legal Sector Affinity Group).

The main AML requirements are set out in the Money Laundering, Terrorist Financing and Transfer of Funds (Information on the Payer) Regulations 2017 ('the Regulations') (as amended by the Money Laundering and Terrorist Financing (Amendment) Regulations 2019 and the Money Laundering and Terrorist Financing (Amendment) (EU Exit) Regulations 2020). It is unlikely that you will have to quote these in your everyday conveyancing work but it is important for you to know the name of the relevant Regulations. Note that the previous Regulations were dated 2007; if your firm's standard letters or reports still refer to the 2007 version, they should be updated because the 2017 version came into force on 10 January 2020.

In broad terms, organisations must assess the risk of money-laundering and take steps to decrease the risk that money coming into the organisation is the proceeds of crime. Firms must carry out a Practice Wide Risk Assessment to assess the risk of money laundering to that particular organisation. From this firm must produce its AML Policies, Controls and Procedures (PCPs) which sets out the overarching AML governance arrangements of the practice. The PCPs must include the firms' requirements regarding issues such as client due diligence procedures, identification and verification procedures and procedures to understand source of funds and source of wealth (see below).

AML Guidance

The LSAG comprises the AML supervisors for the legal sector and includes the SRA and CLC. The LSAG produced guidance on the regulations in January 2021 which made some significant changes to the way law firms will deal with AML requirements and risks. Firms should by now have reviewed the LSAG Guidance and considered updating the firm's PCPs. An integral part of the guidance is to ensure that all staff receive regular and appropriate training on AML risks and requirements.

Practice Points

Every firm should have a Practice Wide Risk Assessment which is an assessment of the risks presented to the firm taking account the type of work that they do and the type of clients that they act for. Senior people in the firm should prepare this document. The LSAG Guidance states that to enable firms to take a risk-based approach to the risk of money-laundering and terrorist financing, the firm should also have:

client risk assessments which should identify and assess the money laundering and terrorist financing risks identified at individual client levels; and

matter risk assessments which should be carried out on each new matter for a client (particularly where risks are new or non-repetitive)

Conveyancers should be aware of their firm's risk assessment procedures and the firm's requirements regarding issues such as identification and source of funds/wealth.

Personnel in a conveyancing firm

Law firms must have a Money Laundering Reporting Officer (MLRO) who has responsibility for ensuring that the firm complies with the Regulations and that any suspicious activity is properly reported. It is essential for all conveyancers to know who holds the role of MLRO in their firm.

In addition, depending on the size of the firm, law firms should have a Money Laundering Compliance Officer (MLCO) who has responsibility for the firm's compliance with its PCPs to stop, detect and prevent money laundering (as appropriate to the size and nature of the firm). The MLCO must be someone senior in the firm.

Money laundering and conveyancing

It is impossible to overstate the importance of money-laundering in a conveyancing context because the risk is consistently high. The combined effect of a firm's PCPs and its frontline staff should be to try to stop dirty money being paid into client account in the first place. Conveyancing is a prime target for criminals simply due to the volume of money which can pass through a firm's client account on any given day.

Every conveyancing firm should have its own policies to help staff recognise risky transactions and the possibility of money-laundering. The following are some of the more common warning signs of money-laundering in a conveyancing context:

- a buyer who is purchasing with cash (that is, not taking out any mortgage financing to fund the purchase)
- payments coming into the conveyancing firm from a number of different individuals or sources
- money being paid into the conveyancing firm from a party other than the client of the firm
- multiple owners of a property
- a foreign element
- sudden or unexplained changes in ownership of property
- an unusual sale price
- an unwillingness by the client to prove identity
- a client who is anxious to pay over funds for a prospective transaction, before it is requested, unless there is a justifiable reason. A simple way to launder money is to pay money to a conveyancer ostensibly being a large deposit for a house purchase or some other transaction, which is quickly cancelled. The client therefore asks for their money back from the conveyancer and the illegal money has been 'cleaned' through the firm's client account
- a situation where money is paid direct between the seller and buyer and not via the conveyancing firms

Know Your Client

The Law Society, SRA and CLC all have resources and information on their websites regarding the risks of money-laundering and how conveyancing firms can recognise and mitigate these risks.

In addition to looking out for potential risky transactions, conveyancing firms must know their clients, often referred to as 'KYC' (know your client). This involves a combination of factors including:

- **the need for the firm to carry out appropriate identification and verification procedures** – in addition to obtaining evidence of the client's identity (such as, passport, driving licence and utility bills) many conveyancing firms will also carry out online electronic checks to further verify that their client is who they purport to be (see further below)

- **the need for the firm to verify 'beneficial owners' of a client** – if a client is a limited company (which is a separate legal entity) the firm must establish the individuals who are behind the company and carry out appropriate identification and verification procedures of those people

- **the need for the firm to obtain information on the purpose of the client's business relationship with the firm and the purpose of the underlying transaction** – this involves obtaining further information and asking questions of the client. Look out for a client who is not interested in the transaction, or who is secretive or vague – this could suggest that they are trying to hide something. Every client wants their conveyancing transaction to move quickly but if a client is pushing very hard for a speedy transaction or seems reluctant to give information, this could be a further red flag. Do not underestimate the importance of basic questions to a conveyancing client such as:

'Why are you selling this property?'

'Why are you buying this property?'

'What is the purpose of this transaction?'

Identifying the client

Whether a firm is regulated by the SRA or CLC, it is necessary to carry out appropriate due diligence to identify the client. This generally means requiring the client to produce sufficient documentary evidence that the firm can be reasonably sure that the person instructing them is genuine and not a fraudster.

In addition to the regulatory requirements, law firms also need to carry out identification checks to comply with AML obligations and obligations imposed by the Lender's Handbook (see Chapter 7). The

Court of Appeal also confirmed that a firm acting for the buyer of a property is entitled to rely on the confirmation from a seller's conveyancing firm that the seller of a property is the true owner (*Dreamvar*). This point was reinforced in the Code for Completion by Post (2019), which we will mention in Chapter 8.

Accordingly, the importance for a conveyancing firm of having strict processes in place to carry out identification of a client cannot be overstated. Everyone working in a conveyancing department must understand that carrying out these identification checks is not just a tiresome administration task. It is central to the creation of the retainer between the firm and the client. Other firms and lenders are entitled to rely on the fact that a firm has carried out proper identification checks. If a firm does not do so and a party to the transaction, the law firm on the other side or a lender loses money as a result of the actions of a fraudster, the firm acting for the fraudster is likely to have to meet the losses incurred from its Professional Indemnity Insurance.

The detail of what documents or electronic checks might be appropriate is beyond the scope of this Practical Guide. We are aiming to give an overview of the key principles and risks. The documentation or checks will differ depending on whether the client is a natural person or a limited company, for example, and the attitude to risk of the particular conveyancing firm. The process of trying to establish that the client is who they say they are is often referred to as 'identity and verification' and this is part of the process of Client Due Diligence (CDD). Before we move on, there are another couple of acronyms to understand:

> **PEP** – this refers to a Politically Exposed Person. The Law Society defines a PEP as 'someone who has been appointed by a community institution, an international body or a state, including the UK, to a high-profile position within the last 12 months. Under the AML Regulations, the main aim of applying additional scrutiny to work involving PEPs is to mitigate the risk that the proceeds of bribery and corruption may be laundered, or assets otherwise stripped from their country of origin.' Examples of PEPs are: MPs, members of governing bodies of political parties. The definition of PEP also includes their family

members. If someone is identified as a PEP, it is necessary for the firm to carry out EDD.

EDD – this refers to Enhanced Due Diligence. As the name implies, this is the process of applying more thorough checks and investigations to a higher risk client and goes beyond the CDD steps.

Let's look at what the various organisations say regarding identifying clients:

SRA – Code of Conduct for Solicitors

Rule 8.1 – *you identify who you are acting for relation to any matter*

CLC – Anti-Money Laundering & Combating Terrorist Financing Code

Rule 11(a) – *you establish the client's identity, obtaining proof of that identity to establish that a client is who they say they are and that they live at the address given*

Lender's Handbook

Section 3 of the Lender's Handbook sets out the safeguards which SRA and CLC regulated firms must comply with. In both cases it requires firms to follow the rules and guidance of their professional body relating to money laundering.

In relation to SRA regulated firms, the Lender's Handbook goes on to say at para 3.1.5 that *'unless you personally know the signatory of a document, you must ask the signatory to provide evidence of identity, which you must carefully check. You should check the signatory's identity against one of the documents from list A law to the documents in list B:*

List A

- *a valid full passport; or*

- *a valid H M Forces identity card with the signatory's photograph; or*

- *a valid UK Photo-card driving licence; or*

- *any other document listed in the additional list A in part 2.*

List B

- *a cheque guarantee card, credit card (bearing the Mastercard or Visa logo) American Express or Diners Club card, debit or multi-function card (bearing the Switch or Delta logo) issued in the United Kingdom with an original account statement less than three months old; or*

- *a firearm and shot gun certificate; or*

- *a receipted utility bill less than three months old; or*

- *a council tax bill less than three months old; or*

- *a council rent book showing the rent paid for the last three months; or*

- *a mortgage statement from another lender for the mortgage accounting year just ended; or*

- *any other document listed in the additional list B in part 2.*

Para 3.16 states:

'You should check that any document you use to verify a signatory's identity appears to be authentic and current, signed in the relevant place. You should take a copy of it and keep the copy on your file. You should also check that the signatory's signature on any document being used to verify identity matches the signatory's signature on the document we require the signatory to sign and that the address shown on any document used to verify identity is that of the signatory.'

The safeguards for CLC regulated firms in the Lender's Handbook are as follows:

Para 3.2.5:

'Unless you personally know the signatory of a document, you must ask the signatory to provide evidence of identity, which you must carefully check. You must satisfy yourself that the person signing the document is the borrower, mortgagor or guarantor (as appropriate). If you have any concerns about the identity of the signatory you should notify us immediately.'

Para 3.2.6:

'You should check that any document you use to verify a signatory's identity appears to be authentic and current, signed in the relevant place. You should take a copy of it and keep the copy on your file. You should also check that the signatory's signature on any document being used to verify identity matches the signatory's signature on the document we require the signatory to sign and that the address shown on any document used to verify identity is that of the signatory.'

Paper identification documents or electronic?

You will see that the regulators and the lenders are not particularly specific as to what steps firms must take in relation to identifying their clients and what documents they should obtain. This is to pass the responsibility for this issue onto the firms. Every conveyancing firm will have its own requirements as to what is acceptable in terms of identification documents. It is up to everyone working in that conveyancing department to understand its firm's requirements.

Some firms will require clients to attend the office to produce originals of the documents in lists A and B above for photocopying and handing back to the client. Some firms will require clients to personally attend with their own documents and will not accept identification documents produced by anyone else (for example, a spouse of the client). Generally, any documents which are photocopied will be certified by the firm as true copies of the original. These should be dated and the person who has taken the copies should sign and print their name together with that of the firm.

Many firms will subscribe to additional electronic checks which will be carried out against the name of all clients instructing the firm. There are a number of different providers of such services which will generally carry out a search of electronic databases against the name of the client. The checks usually use public information and private databases and the client will often need to provide their date of birth, address, National Insurance number and/or passport number. Central to any electronic checks, therefore, is ensuring that the correct name is searched against. This might sound obvious but in its AML guidance, the LSAG Guidance states (our emphasis):

'As technology has developed, use of electronic identification and verification (EID&V) tools have become more common. While you can never outsource your ultimate responsibility, EID&V tools can be useful in protecting your practice. (para 6.14.3)

In an increasingly digital age, it is clear that non face-to-face customer onboarding can no longer be viewed as always high risk (although it remains a key risk factor to be assessed in the context of the wider relationship) – a more nuanced approach should therefore be adopted to these types of relationships.

...

EID&V is also sensitive to human error, and mistakes of data input can lead to the incorrect individual being checked. *Practices should consider the risks of this and how they mitigate, e.g., dip sampling past files to check accuracy, ideally by another individual at the practice. Practices should also be alert to any surprising results that may indicate human error at the data input stage. It is not acceptable to simply run a search on a prospective or current client and file it as having completed the identification and verification process, without consideration of the wider risks (see Section 5). Practice units must bear in mind that identification and verification is one element of overall customer due diligence requirements necessary under the Regulations. (para 7.3)'*

A word on *Dreamvar*

The LSAG Guidance makes it clear that any electronic system is only as good as the person inputting the information or considering the result of the search. For example, in *Dreamvar,* which is a case involving a fraudulent seller, an AML search was done but it came back as "Referred" because it was not possible to "uniquely identify the applicant at his address". Unsurprisingly, it was also impossible to verify the name of the fraudulent seller's date of birth from the available databases including the electoral roll. Notwithstanding this, the person handling the file made no further attempts to verify the fraudulent seller's identity and accepted him as a client. Had the problem with the AML search result been identified and dealt with, the whole fraud and ensuing Court of Appeal case might never have happened.

Practice Points

All conveyancing firms should have their own requirements as to what is acceptable in terms of client identification contained in a policy document. There are additional, different requirements if the client is a limited company or a trust. Different firms will have different attitudes to identification documents which have been certified by another firm or organisation. The onset of the Covid 19 pandemic has also presented additional challenges in relation to identifying clients because it has often not been possible to meet clients face-to-face.

All of the above challenges represent risks to conveyancing firms. It is the responsibility of everyone in a conveyancing department to understand the requirements of their particular firm and if in doubt as to the client, the documents produced or the result of any online electronic verification, further guidance should be obtained from a qualified colleague or the firm's MLRO.

Many firms have a zero tolerance approach to due diligence in that they will not allow any work to be carried out on the file until all due diligence aspects have been dealt with including identification and source of wealth and source of funds checks.

Source of funds and source of wealth

The key risk to conveyancers is receiving large sums of money from clients. Firms must consider where the money is coming from on every purchase transaction and a good starting point is to consider the level of risk:

- Low risk – property funded from proceeds of sale, and/or mortgage
- Medium risk – property funded form proceeds of sale, and/or mortgage and savings
- High risk – purchases being funded from substantial private funds; 3rd party funding; complicated funding arrangements; corporate or overseas funding

'A fundamental element of client due diligence is understanding the nature, background and circumstances of the client, including their financial position – and making an assessment as to whether the legal services provided to the

client are in keeping with your understanding of that background and circumstances. The extent to which you must obtain, review and evidence your client's financial position is dependent upon the risk profile of the client or matter. In enhanced due diligence situations this requirement is more stringent.' (LSAG Guidance para 6.17)

SRA research has shown that some conveyancing firms remain unclear as to the differential between source of funds and source of wealth. The LSAG Guidance states as follows:

*'**Source of Funds** refers to the funds that are being used to fund the specific transaction in hand – i.e., the origin of the funds used for the transactions or activities that occur within the business relationship or occasional transaction. The question you are seeking to answer should not simply be, "where did the money for the transaction come from," but also "how and from where did the client get the money for this transaction or business relationship." It is not enough to know the money came from a UK bank account.'* (Para 6.17.2)

Every firm should specify in its PCPs what evidence is acceptable for source of funds but examples include:

- client bank statements
- a will and/or estate accounts if the funds are an inheritance for payslips
- audited accounts
- sale/purchase agreements
- receipts of other transactions
- establishing income from share capital, business activities etc

*'The **source of wealth** refers to the origin of a client's entire body of wealth (i.e., total assets). SoW describes the economic, business and/or commercial activities that generated, or significantly contributed to, the client's overall net worth/entire body of wealth. This should recognise that the composition of wealth generating activities may change over time, as new activities are identified, and additional wealth is accumulated. You should seek to answer the question: "why and how does the individual have the amount of overall assets they do – and how did they accumulate/generate these?"'* (LSAG Guidance para 6.17.3)

Each conveyancing firm will set out in its PCPs what evidence is acceptable to establish source of wealth. This can be a complex financial task/review and in the event that a conveyancer feels unsure as to how to assess any evidence produced by the client, they should refer to an immediate superior and/or the firm's MLRO. The purpose is to *build a rationale and reasoning as to why [the client has] such wealth and to provide assurance that it was obtained through legal means'* (LSAG Guidance para 6.18.3).

Put simply, source of funds seeks to establish where is the client's money now, which will typically be in a bank account in the client's name. Source of wealth seeks to establish where that money came from. It cannot be assumed that all conveyancing firms carry out these checks and procedures. The SRA carried out a review which, alarmingly, revealed that some firms *'had difficulties separating the concepts of source of funds and source of wealth, and did not distinguish them'*. As part of this research exercise, the SRA produced a summary which firms might find useful because it contains self-assessment questions for firms in relation to AML policies and procedures and ways that firms could consider how to develop and improve: SRA – *Preventing Money Laundering and Financing of Terrorism – Summary report March 2018*

Link: https://www.sra.org.uk/globalassets/documents/sra/research/preventing-money-laundering-summary.pdf?version=4a1ac3

What if the funds are coming from a third-party?

The most obvious example of this is a 'gifted deposit' in a conveyancing transaction, for example, parents are making a gift of some money to the firm's client to assist with a purchase. This is a common occurrence these days. The LSAG Guidance states as follows: *'In circumstances where a client declares that they have been given funds for a transaction from a third party you may wish to record information relating to that original transaction too. You may verify this by requesting bank statements and other relevant documentation relating to this transfer'* (para 6.17.2.1).

Many conveyancing firms will have additional requirements in their PCPs to deal with funds coming from a third-party including obtaining identification documents for that third-party.

Practice Points

Conveyancers must avoid the possibility of a third-party (for example, parents gifting a deposit) thinking that the firm is also acting for them because the firm has requested their identification documents. The conveyancer must make it clear that the only purpose for requesting identification documents and evidence as to source of funds/wealth is for the purposes of AML due diligence in relation to the client of the firm. A conveyancing firm should avoid acting for the third-party due to the significant risk of a conflict-of-interest arising.

What if the funds are coming from abroad?

If the client provides evidence that any money is coming from a non-UK based bank account, the firm should adopt a more stringent approach to source of funds and source of wealth. The general concern is that money does not come into a firm from a jurisdiction which does not have comparable AML regulations to the UK. The LSAG Guidance refers to a list of 'high risk third countries' and there is also a 'sanctions list' which details countries where the risk in relation to money laundering is higher. The Guidance makes it clear that prohibited in clients from outside the UK or that are not UK nationals is not a requirement of the money laundering regulations (5.6.2.1). The point is to ensure that the firm has appropriate due diligence procedures in place to identify the risk and be satisfied as to the source of funds. Country risk factors should appear in the firm's Practice Wide Risk Assessment.

Conveyancers should also understand their firm's requirements in relation to assets such as bitcoin and crypto currency.

Practice Points

The fairly straightforward rule that someone in a conveyancing team can always apply is that if it is evident from the information provided by the client that their money is anywhere other than in a UK based bank account, the conveyancer should make further enquiries or ask a qualified professional or the firm's Money Laundering Reporting Officer before confirming the retainer or accepting money into client account.

What if the client wants you to send money abroad?

Many conveyancing firms have a straightforward requirement that any money being sent by the firm to the client (for example, the net sale proceeds on completion of a sale transaction) must be sent to a UK based bank account in the name of the client. Again, it is not against the Regulations for a firm to send money abroad but it does expose the firm to a higher level of risk.

Client account must not be used as a banking facility

A related issue is the fact that a regulatory requirement is that law firms should not allow their client account to be used as a banking facility for their clients. In broad terms, this means that on completion of a sale, for example, the firm should send the net sale proceeds direct to the client's bank account and not to other parties or accounts requested by the client.

Firms must only accept money into their client account where there is a proper connection between receipt of the funds and the delivery by the firm of regulated legal services. When paying money out of client account, the SRA advises that firms should always ask themselves why they are being asked to make a payment or why the client cannot make all received payment directly themselves. They sum up rather neatly as follows:

'The client's convenience is not a legitimate reason, nor is not having access to a bank account in the UK. '

(SRA Warning Notice – Improper use of client account as a banking facility. Link: https://www.sra.org.uk/solicitors/guidance/improper-client-account-banking-facility/)

Money laundering myths

Conveyancing firms should not make any assumptions about their client's or their money. It might be tempting to make some seemingly obvious assumptions to speed up the due diligence procedures at the beginning of a transaction, but this must be avoided! Some common myths are:

> If a client's money is already in a UK based bank account it must be 'clean' and the firm does not need to check it – myth!

Conveyancing firms cannot assume that UK banks check the source of deposits. The Financial Conduct Authority fined HSBC Bank plc £63.9m for *'failings in its anti-money laundering processes'*. (Source: www.fca.org.uk, Dec 2021)

Money-laundering must involve an international element – myth! Money-laundering can involve seemingly mundane processes such as not paying tax to HMRC or defrauding money from an employer.

Money-laundering could not happen to our firm, we are a local High Street firm – myth! Fraudsters will target smaller, local firms perhaps assuming that their AML procedures are not as robust.

A conveyancing firm can rely on identification documents certified by another professional organisation – myth! It is up to each firm to determine the level of risk that it is prepared to take but a firm will not automatically be protected if documents certified by another organisation subsequently turn out to be fraudulent.

A conveyancing firm only has to check the client's identity; there is no obligation to ask about the source of funds – myth! As we have seen above, enquiring as to source of funds and source of wealth is a central part of AML due diligence.

A conveyancing firm must prove that a client's money is clean – myth! A conveyancing firm is required to consider whether the source of funds and wealth is consistent with the risk profile of the client, the retainer and their business.

The Law Society has produced a helpful 'top tips' sheet which conveyancers can download to assist with AML monitoring.

Link: https://www.lawsociety.org.uk/Topics/Property/Guides/anti-money-laundering-in-property (scroll down to 'keep a record' where you will find a link to the PDF)

Practice Points

Conveyancers must understand what to do in the event that they are concerned about a client's source of funds/wealth or simply have a suspicion or uncomfortable feeling about a client. There are a number of do's and don'ts which will help to mitigate the risk of the firm being a victim of money-laundering:

- understand your firm's PCPs in relation to these matters

- understand whether you are permitted to carry out any work on a client file before all of the AML, identification and due diligence procedures are satisfactorily concluded

- if a firm uses an electronic third-party verification tool, ensure that it is used properly and correctly on every client. The LSAG Guidance points out a basic, but important risk here, that of human error, it is *'sensitive to human error, and mistakes of data input can lead to the incorrect individual being checked'* (para 7.3)

- under no circumstances should any suspicions or concerns be shared with the client – this could amount to 'tipping off' which would alert the client to the firm's suspicions and which in itself is an offence

- know whom to ask in the event of a question/problem – either go to an immediate superior or the firm's MLRO

- act immediately – share concerns with the appropriate person in the firm at the earliest possible opportunity

- do not share any suspicions or concerns with anyone outside the firm, whether a partner/ spouse of the client, estate agent, mortgage broker or other conveyancer

- do not attempt to report any concern – if a conveyancer has any questions about a client's identification documents, source of funds/wealth or any other matter, this should be reported to the MLRO. It is the role of the MLRO to make a 'Suspicious Activity Report' (SAR) to the National Crime Agency (NCA) if there is an ongoing concern – the individual conveyancer should not do this

- do not see identification, verification and risk assessment as a one-off task to be completed at the beginning of a transaction. It is an ongoing responsibility throughout the life of a matter

- ensure that all steps taken and decisions made in relation to these matters are properly noted on the file

- a conveyancing firm is not obliged to take on a client or their transaction, so if a firm has a continued suspicion about a client, they could decline to act

- AML, identification and due diligence procedures are not just 'administration'. They are an integral part of the conveyancing process which assist in protecting the firm from fraud and money laundering

- AML, identification and due diligence procedures are everyone's job!

- if in doubt – ask! In the majority of cases, a suspicion about a client's activities will not result in a finding of money laundering but conveyancers must be encouraged to trust their instincts and share concerns with the appropriate person in the firm

Fraud risks

We have considered risks in relation to money laundering in particular. However, conveyancing firms must be constantly vigilant to the risks of fraud. Other examples include:

A fraudulent seller

A fraudster may set themselves up as the 'seller' of a property that they do not own. If a firm's identification and KYC procedures are weak, this type of fraud could involve a firm acting for a buyer sending the purchase money (which could include a mortgage advance from a lender) to the seller's conveyancer who sends the money to a fraudster rather than the true seller. By the time the fraud is discovered, the fraudster is likely to have absconded with the money. This is broadly what happened in the *Dreamvar* case. As mentioned above, following this case, the Law Society reaffirmed that a buyer's conveyancer is entitled to rely on a seller's conveyancer confirming that the person purporting to be the seller is the true owner of the property. This was confirmed in the Code for Completion by Post (2019) – see Chapter 8.

Warning signs of this type of fraud include:

- the only contact details for the client being a mobile member and/or email address
- where a firm is instructed by more than one person but meets only one party to a transaction
- obvious typographical errors or alterations in documents presented as utility bills (for identification purposes)
- the client being unable or unwilling to provide documentation linking them to the address
- changes to the clients contact details or bank account to which the sale proceeds are to be sent

Impersonation of a law firm and identity theft

Conveyancing firms have been held liable for losses incurred by fraud resulting from situations where fraudsters have set themselves up as either a bogus law firm or a non-existent branch office of a well-known, large law firm. In both cases, the legitimate law firm thinks they are sending purchase money to a real law firm but, in fact, it is being sent to a fraudster.

Practice Points

You will no doubt recognise some of the steps that conveyancing firms can take to mitigate the risk of this type of fraud including:

- using an electronic checking service to confirm that the law firm or office exists
- checking a firm's website to ensure that a branch office exists
- insisting on receiving at least some communication from the firm via the post as opposed to all correspondence being by email
- telephoning the senior partner of the firm to ensure that a branch office exists
- checking that the law firm on the other side is on record with, for example, the SRA, CLC or other legal regulatory body is practising at the address provided (note that this is a specific requirement in section 3 (safeguards) of the Lender's Handbook)

- checking with the SRA, CLC or other legal regulatory body that the that the fee earner dealing with the transaction is a recognised, regulated individual (e.g., by using the Law Society's 'Find a Solicitor' service)

Mortgage fraud

Mortgage fraud happens when a person deliberately gives incorrect information to a lender to obtain a mortgage. The Lender's Handbook imposes significant obligations on the conveyancer acting for the lender to help combat mortgage fraud including:

- making appropriate identity checks (3.1)
- informing the lender if the seller has owned the property for less than 6 months (5.1.1)
- asking the borrower how the balance of the purchase money is being provided and reporting to the lender if it is not coming from the borrower's own funds (5.13.1)
- ensuring there are no discrepancies between the mortgage offer and the documents provided by the seller (6.1.2)
- ensuring that the purchase price is the same in the offer as in the contract (6.3)
- reporting any incentives to the lender on a new build (using the UK Finance Disclosure of Incentives Form) (6.4.1)

Cyber threats

The risk of falling victim to cybercrime is a constant concern for conveyancing firms and is at the top of the agenda for regulators and professional indemnity insurers. Conveyancing firms are especially at risk due to the amount of money that passes through client account. Conveyancers and their clients must mitigate the risk of paying money over to fraudsters. Two of the most common types of cyber threat for firms are:

1. **email modification fraud** – this is the situation where criminals intercept emails and remove legitimate bank account details and replace them with the fraudster's account details

2. **phishing** – this is the situation where criminals trick victims into handing over sensitive information or installing malware. The two main methods are either a malicious email attachment which installs malware on the victim's machine when it is opened or links to malicious websites

Practice Points

It is essential that organisations provide regular training on cybercrime risks for everyone in their firm. One of the problems with cybercrime is that the risk is always present so busy staff can easily forget about or ignore the risks.

Common procedures which conveyancing firms put in place are:

- wording on all email footers indicating that the firm's bank account details will not change
- a procedure to verify the recipient and check bank account details of the recipient every time a telegraphic transfer is sent out (this is particularly important on completion – see Chapter 8)
- a policy that the firm's bank account details will not be sent to anyone outside the firm by email (even as a PDF attachment)
- training staff to be cautious about emails received that seem unusual or have poor spelling and grammar
- training staff to avoid opening unsolicited emails with links and attachments
- ensuring that staff know whom to contact in the event that a suspicious communication is received or, worse, a problem is identified or a suspicious link is opened

Home and remote working have increased the risks and conveyancing staff must ensure that they comply with their firms remote working and own device policies which should cover issues such as:

- password protocols
- mobile working policy relating to safe use of systems and devices
- understanding the policy on using removable media
- complying with protocols relating to unsecure Wi-Fi

The National Cyber Security Centre has a really useful free e-learning package called 'Top Tips for Staff'. Link:

https://www.ncsc.gov.uk/training/top-tips-for-staff-scorm-v2/scormcontent/index.html#/

Red flag checklists

The LSAG Guidance lists over 200 issues which should concern law firms in relation to money laundering. More generally, conveyancing firms should consider the transactional risks which may arise on a particular file. If these factors are identified on a file, this should act as a 'red flag' to the conveyancer prompting them to assess the risks more carefully on the file. To assist conveyancers, firms may require their conveyancing department to use a 'red flag checklist' to help identify risky files.

The identification of red flags on a file does not mean that the firm should cease to act but rather that the conveyancer should be more careful and conduct additional checks whether on the funds, the property, parties or EDD on the client.

Examples of red flags in conveyancing

There are far too many red flags to detail. The presence of one or more red flags denotes a potential risk in relation to that transaction which the conveyancer should consider and act upon. Examples of red flag risks in conveyancing which you might commonly encounter include:

- a cash transaction
- the client not being local to your firm and not providing a reasonable explanation as to why they have chosen your firm
- an empty property (for example because the owner has died)
- a high value property
- a property with no mortgage
- a property that is let (tenanted)
- foreign element (e.g. client is abroad or they want the money sent abroad)
- unexplained urgency
- not meeting the client face to face

- seller's address not the same as the property being sold

The CLC has produced a useful AML red flags checklist. Link:

https://www.clc-uk.org/anti-money-laundering-red-flags/

Practice Points

There is a dizzying array of risk and information for busy conveyancers to keep in mind. Some of the most important advice is to always ask 'does it all add up?'. Follow your instinct. If something feels wrong, it probably is. The key thing is to not alert the client or any other party to any concerns (at worst, this could amount to the money-laundering offence of 'tipping off'). Always know who to ask in your firm if you think that there is a problem.

And remember…

The AML checks and source of funds and source of wealth investigations together with the identification and other checks discussed in this Chapter are all part of the due diligence requirements relating to Know Your Client (KYC). A firm's Policies and Procedures (PCPs) should all be designed to assist those in the conveyancing department to adopt a risk-based assessment to enable the firm to be reasonably sure that the client is who they say they are and that any money which they are putting into a property transaction is not the product of criminal activity.

Conveyancers must consider AML, due diligence regarding funds and client identification at the beginning of a transaction to decide whether or not to create the retainer and carry out the work for the client. However, being on the alert for all of these issues is a continuing obligation throughout the transaction and is not something that is concluded once the file is opened.

CHAPTER FOUR
TITLE TO LAND

We have seen that central to the conveyancing process is establishing that the seller 'owns' the property that they are selling. We have also seen that a person does not, strictly, 'own' land but, rather, must demonstrate that they hold one of the two legal estates in land, either freehold or leasehold. Having a legal estate is described as having 'title' to the land and it is the job of the conveyancers to deal with the transfer of title. In this Chapter we will look at how the seller proves their title to the land that they are selling.

At the beginning of the conveyancing transaction, the seller's conveyancer must obtain evidence of the seller's title to their land and must draft the contract for the sale of land (see Chapter 6). The process of demonstrating title to land is called 'deducing title'. Upon receipt of the contract pack, one of the main tasks for the buyer's conveyancer is to check that the seller's title is acceptable. This is known as 'investigating title'. If the buyer's conveyancer has any questions or concerns about the seller's title, these will be raised as part of the buyers 'pre-contract enquiries' (see Chapter 7). The buyer's conveyancer should not exchange contracts until all of these enquiries and matters of title have been answered to their satisfaction.

As we will see in Chapter 8, after completion, the buyer's conveyancer must register the transfer of title from the seller to the buyer with HMLR (plus any mortgage that the buyer has taken out to fund the purchase). If there are any problems which remain unresolved on completion, it will then be up to the buyer's conveyancer to try to resolve them, which could prove difficult.

Although this Practical Guide is dealing predominantly with the much more common registered title, we do still need to mention the traditional form of title to land, that of unregistered title. As we will see, the process of registering land in England and Wales has taken place incrementally since 1925. Most of the land mass of England and Wales is now registered but there are still pockets of unregistered land meaning that conveyancing firms must be able to deal with both registered and unregistered titles.

Unregistered title

Proving title to land by producing documentary evidence of ownership is the traditional method of deducing title to land. If the title is unregistered, a seller must produce documentary evidence which goes back at least 15 years showing an unbroken ownership from the first document (called the 'root of title') to the current seller. Investigating an unregistered title and identifying and appropriate root of title is a specialist area which a conveyancer who does not have the appropriate experience should not carry out.

The unregistered title deeds are the only evidence of the seller's ownership therefore the seller's conveyancer will retain the original documents and will only send copies to the buyer's conveyancer with the contract. The seller's conveyancer will prepare an 'epitome of title' which is a chronological list of the relevant documents of title, together with photocopies of those documents attached to it.

It can be seen that one of the key risks with the unregistered system is that the title deeds might get lost. This is one of the main reasons why the system of land registration that exists today was set up. HMLR was originally set up under the terms of the LRA 1925. This Act was repealed by the LRA 2002.

HMLR is the government agency which is responsible for dealing with land registration in England and Wales. There are 14 HMLR offices around the country although a significant proportion of its daily business is now carried out electronically via the portal. The Land Register contains more than 26 million titles showing evidence of ownership for more than 87% of the land mass of England and Wales.

In essence, the purpose of land registration is to distil of the relevant information about the title to the property and to create a computerised register of title. Once a title to land is registered, the unregistered title deeds no longer have any legal significance. After registration, any subsequent dealing with the land must be registered with HMLR so that the register of title can be updated. It is still possible to submit paper applications for registration to HMLR but most conveyancing firms will use the HMLR portal to upload applications electronically. A conveyancing firm must have a contract with HMLR to enable it to use the portal facility and HMLR's fees for registration are taken direct from the firm via direct debit on a monthly basis.

Practice Points

Conveyancers will often encounter an unregistered title is days where the owner has died (a probate sale). It may be necessary to give an undertaking to a lender to release the unregistered title deeds to the conveyancing firm to enable the sale to proceed. It is imperative that a bundle of unregistered title deeds is stored safely in the firm's strongroom and the deeds must not be released to the buyer's conveyancer until such time as completion has taken place. Remember, with an unregistered title, there is no convenient, computerised register of title in existence. Accordingly, the only evidence of ownership is the unregistered deeds and they must be stored securely and treated with respect.

When must an unregistered title be registered at HMLR?

An unregistered title must be registered at HMLR when one of the events that 'triggers' first registration takes place. Since 1 December 1990, the whole of England and Wales is subject to compulsory first registration meaning that when a triggering event takes place, an application to register the unregistered title at HMLR must be made. The most common triggering events in a freehold context are: the sale of a property, the gift of a property and an assent of property to a beneficiary out of the estate of someone who has died. Also, if a property owner is mortgaging all or part of an unregistered title, the land being mortgaged must be registered.

The application for first registration must be made to HMLR using form FR1 within two months of completion of the triggering event. In essence, evidence of the unregistered title is sent to HMLR and they review the title submitted to them. If it is acceptable, HMLR will create a register of title.

The class of title

When an application for first registration is made, HMLR will investigate the title and if it is acceptable, the title will be registered and the class of title will be allocated. There are various classes of title which HMLR can issue, the most common of which are as follows:

absolute freehold title – this is the best class of title available

possessory title – this is a class of title based on physical possession of the land rather than documentary evidence. HMLR might issue this class of title if the application for registration is based on someone using the land unchallenged (often referred to as a 'squatter') or if the unregistered title deeds have been lost

qualified title – this is rarely encountered in practice

There are also classes of title relevant to a leasehold estate which are beyond the scope of this Practical Guide.

Registration of a title at HMLR confers a state guarantee of title. This means that every registered title is backed up by indemnity if a mistake is made in the register that causes loss.

Practice Points

When investigating a registered title, a conveyancer acting for a buyer will always want to see title absolute. If you see possessory title when acting for a buyer or lender, always raise it with a qualified practitioner. Exchange of contracts should not take place until this has been satisfactorily addressed. It is possible to upgrade a possessory title to title absolute if the registered proprietor can demonstrate to HMLR that the possessory title has not been challenged for 12 years since it was granted. Alternatively, indemnity insurance might be required (see Chapter 5). In either case, this is a risk to a buyer and their conveyancer and is an issue which the seller and their conveyancer should be required to resolve prior to exchange of contracts. Remember, if a buyer's conveyancer completes on behalf of their client and there is a problem, it is then up to the buyer's conveyancer to resolve it which might prove difficult.

What does the register of title contain?

We have seen that the process of land registration effectively distils the relevant, current information about the title to a property and that information is recorded on a computerised register of title which is maintained by HMLR. What are the most important things that we need to know about a property? We need to know:

- whether the property is freehold leasehold
- the address of the property
- whether there are any easements (rights) which benefit the property
- who holds the legal title to the property
- the class of title
- whether there are any mortgages affecting the property
- whether there are any covenants or other interests which affect the property

Let's look at an example of a fictitious register of title for the above information. The whole register is below and we will then break it down and look at it in stages. The register contains entries which you will commonly encounter although not necessarily all in the same register of title.

The explanation of the parts of the register tells you how to investigate a register of title.

Official copy of register of title	Title number SK98765	Edition date 06.08.2019

- This official copy shows the entries on the register of title on 29 September 2021 at 10.34.10.
- This date must be quoted as the "search from date" in any official search application based on this copy.
- The date at the beginning of an entry is the date on which the entry was made in the register.
- Issued on 06 September 2021.
- Under s.67 of the Land Registration Act 2002, this copy is admissible in evidence to the same extent as the original.
- This title is dealt with by Land Registry Weymouth Office.

A: Property Register

This register describes the land and estate comprised in the title

BERKSHIRE : READING

1 (02.11.2001) The Freehold land shown edged
  with red on the plan of the above title filed
  at the Registry and being School House, The
  Green, Barnford, Berkshire BR5 6YH

2 (02.11.2001) The land has the benefit of a
  right of way contained in a Conveyance dated

10 June 1986 the route of which is shown coloured brown on the title plan

B: Proprietorship Register

This register specifies the class of title and identifies the owner. It contains any entries that affect the right of disposal.

Title absolute

1 (18.01.2017) PROPRIETOR(S): SOPHIA CAROL HAYWARD of School House, The Green, Barnford, Berkshire BR5 6YH and 22 High Street, Barnford, Berkshire BR76 9JK

2 (18.01.2017) RESTRICTION. No disposition of the registered estate by the proprietor of the registered estate or by the proprietor of any registered charge, not being a charge registered before the entry of this restriction, is to be registered without a written consent signed by the proprietor for the time being of the Charge dated 10 January 2017 in favour of National Westminster Bank plc referred to in the Charges Register.

3 (18.01.2017) RESTRICTION. No disposition by a sole proprietor of the registered estate (except a trust corporation) under which capital money arises is to be registered unless authorised by an order of the court.

4 (18.01.2017) The price stated to have been paid on 10 January 2017 was £395,000.

5 (18.01.2017) The transfer to the proprietor contains a covenant to observe and perform the covenants referred to in the Charges Register and of indemnity in respect thereof.

6 (06.08.2019) RESTRICTION. No disposition of the registered estate by the proprietor of the registered estate is to be registered without a certificate signed by a conveyancer that that conveyancer is satisfied that the person who executed the document submitted for registration as disponor is the same person as the proprietor.

C: Charges Register

This register contains any charges and other matters that affect the land

1   (02.11.2001) A Conveyance dated 10 May 1985 made between Marcus Franks (1) and Norman Butters (2) contains covenants details of which are contained in the schedule hereto.

2   (02.11.2001) a Conveyance of the land in this title dated 15 November 1942 made between Laurie Trims (1) and Peter Yardley (2) contains covenants. Neither the original conveyance nor a certified copy or an examined abstract was produced on first registration.

3   (02.11.2001) A Conveyance dated 19 March 1989 made between Butters Builders Limited (1) and Amy Newbold (2) contains covenants.

NOTE: Copy filed

4   (18.01.2017) REGISTERED CHARGE dated 10
     January 2017 to secure the moneys including
     the further advances therein mentioned.

5   (18.01.2017) PROPRIETOR: National Westminster
     Bank plc (Co Regn No 929027) of Mortgage
     Centre, PO Box 123, Greenock PA15 1EF

THE SCHEDULE ABOVE REFERRED TO

1.   Not to use the property as anything other
     than a single residential dwelling without
     the written consent of the Vendor or his
     successors in title.

2.   Not to do or cause anything to be done on
     the property which may be or become a
     nuisance or annoyance to the neighbouring
     properties.

END OF REGISTER

Practice Points

An important principle of land registration is transparency. This means that the registers of title and title plans are available to the public. Those working in conveyancing departments will usually have an HMLR username and password which will give them access to the Land Registry portal. Amongst the many services on offer is the ability to download a register of title and the documents referred to in it. There is a process available if a party wants to keep elements of a document private which involves an application to HMLR to exempt a document from the general right to inspect and obtain a copy of it (see HMLR PG57). However, it is relatively rare for conveyancers to use this process.

The fact that the registers are public means that anyone can, for the appropriate fee, obtain details of the registers and what they contain. This means that conveyancers should be careful when sending documents to HMLR for registration or contacting HMLR for guidance. We have seen in Chapter 1 that generally HMLR keeps the detail of the behind-the-scenes beneficial interest in property off the title. Conveyancers should therefore not send a behind-the-scenes declaration of trust to HMLR with a Land Registry application. This document could contain a lot of personal information about the buyers of a property and their finances. If it is sent to HMLR, anyone could obtain a copy of it. Similarly, if you write to HMLR seeking guidance on a particular point and give details of your client the transaction, this communication could be available to anyone who wants to obtain. This is the case even if the declaration of trust or letter in our example does not appear on a register of title.

Accordingly, always think carefully about the documents being sent to HMLR, particularly if they are unusual or not documents that you would typically send with a registration application.

REGISTER	NOTES
Title number SK98765	The title number is the exclusive identification (or reference) number allocated to property in a particular title by HMLR. The contract and the transfer must refer to the title number.
Edition date 06.08.2019	This is the date when the register for this title was last updated. This might be when the land was last sold, when a mortgage was registered or when a restriction or notice was added. Any change to the content of the register results in a new edition being produced. As we will see, this register was last updated when the restriction at entry 6 of the proprietorship register was added.
This official copy shows the entries on the register of title on 29 September 2021 at 10.34.10. **This date must be quoted as the "search from date" in any official search application based on this copy**	This shows the time and date when the official copy was obtained. In most cases, this will be the time and date when it was downloaded from HMLR via the HMLR Portal by the seller's conveyancer. The 'search from' date is very important. As we will see in Chapter 8 it is the date which must be inserted in the official search with priority (OS1) which is carried out by the buyer's conveyancer before completion.
A: Property Register	The Property Register is the first register of title and gives a brief description of the property, indicates whether it is freehold or leasehold and includes details of any rights which BENEFIT the property.

BERKSHIRE : READING	This indicates the county and district within which the property falls.
1(02.11.2001) The Freehold land shown edged with red on the plan of the above title filed at the Registry and being School House, The Green, Barnford, Berkshire BR5 6YH	You will see that each entry on each register is numbered and has a date in brackets. In this case, this date is the date upon which the property was first registered at HMLR.
1(02.11.2001) The **Freehold** land shown edged with red on the plan of the above title filed at the Registry and being **School House, The Green, Barnford, Berkshire BR5 6YH**	You will see that the property is freehold and the address of the property is indicated. You should always ensure that the contract contains the correct estate in land and the exact address as per the property register.
2 (02.11.2001) The land has the benefit of a right of way contained in a Conveyance dated 10 June 1986 the route of which is shown coloured brown on the title plan .	The property register contains rights which benefit the property. In this case, the property benefits from a right-of-way over adjoining land. HMLR might indicate that a copy of the conveyance dated 10 June 1986 can be obtained (by putting 'copy filed' beneath the entry). However, in this case, HMLR has chosen to indicate the route of the right-of-way with brown colouring on the title plan.

B: Proprietorship Register	The second register that HMLR creates is the proprietorship register. This contains various information including the class of title, the name/s of the current holder/s of the legal estate and any restrictions.
Title absolute	This indicates that HMLR allocated to title absolute on first registration of this title which, as we have seen, is the best form of title available.
	Anything other than title absolute should be raised as a pre-contract enquiry with the seller's conveyancer.
1 (18.01.2017) PROPRIETOR(S): SOPHIA CAROL HAYWARD of School House, The Green, Barnford, Berkshire BR5 6YH and 22 High Street, Barnford, Berkshire BR76 9JK	Entry 1 of the proprietorship register was changed on 18 January 2017 which you will see is just after the date of the most recent purchase of the land by Sophia.
	This tells you that the current holder of the legal estate is Sophia Carol Hayward. She is the sole registered proprietor. You will see that she has to addresses for service, both the property and 22 High Street. This might indicate that she does not live at School House and possibly lets it out.
	Note that up to 3 addresses for the registered proprietor/s can be added to the register, one of which can be an email address.
2 (18.01.2017) RESTRICTION. No disposition of the registered estate by the proprietor of the registered estate or by the proprietor of any registered charge, not being a charge	Entry 2 of the proprietorship register was added on the same date as the above entry.
	Restrictions stop HMLR completing the registration of certain transactions (such as transfers, leases or mortgages) unless the conditions specified in the restriction are met.
	This is the wording for the standard lender restriction. You will see from the charges register that Sophia purchased the property with the aid of a mortgage from National Westminster Bank plc.

registered before the entry of this restriction, is to be registered without a **written consent** signed by the proprietor for the time being of the Charge dated 10 January 2017 in favour of National Westminster Bank plc referred to in the Charges Register.	This restriction ensures that the property cannot be sold or another mortgage added without the written consent of National Westminster Bank plc.
3 (18.01.2017) RESTRICTION. No disposition by a sole proprietor of the registered estate (except a trust corporation) under which capital money arises is to be registered unless authorised by an order of the court.	Entry 3 of the proprietorship register was also added at the time of Sophia's purchase. You will recall that this is the standard Form A restriction which you will recall is entered when the owners are trustees. This restriction limits what one registered proprietor can do on their own. This is significant in this case because Sophia is a sole registered proprietor – see Chapter 1.
4 (18.01.2017) The price stated to have been	This type of entry has been included on the register since 1 April 2000. It is taken from the transfer or application form submitted to HMLR on registration. You will see that Sophia's

paid on **10 January 2017** was £395,000	purchase completed on 10 January 2017. HMLR does not verify the price. This just reflects the price paid by the current registered proprietor.
5 (18.01.2017) The transfer to the proprietor contains a covenant to observe and perform the covenants referred to in the Charges Register and of indemnity in respect thereof	This entry is taken from the transfer that is submitted to HMLR for registration of the current registered proprietor. If they have promised to comply with the covenants (that is, obligations) on the charges register of the title, this entry will appear on the proprietorship register. This promise is called an 'indemnity covenant'. Note that a registered proprietor who is selling their property is not entitled to demand that the incoming buyer gives an indemnity covenant in the transfer if they did not give one (see Chapter 8). The way that you can tell is to look at the proprietorship register for this entry.
6 **(06.08.2019)** RESTRICTION. No disposition of the registered estate by the proprietor of the registered estate is to be registered without a certificate signed by a conveyancer that that conveyancer is satisfied that the person who executed the document submitted for registration as	You will note that entry 6 of the proprietorship register has been added at a later date to entries 1 to 5. This is a Form LL restriction. It may have been added to the register using an application on form RQ. It is free to add the restriction to the register and can be added by the registered proprietor at any time. Note that the restriction will not normally be entered by HMLR if the only contract address supplied for the registered proprietor is the address of the property concerned. This would indicate that the individual is living at the property. You will remember that Sophia has two addresses for service. Link to the form: www.gov.uk/government/publications/restriction-by-owner-not-living-at-property-request-registration-rq

`disponor is the same person as the proprietor.`	This restriction helps to guard against fraud. It means that the conveyancer acting for Sophia when she sells must produce a certificate to confirm that they are satisfied that Sophia is the registered proprietor. This certificate should be provided to the buyer's conveyancer on completion. They can then submit the certificate to HMLR with their application for registration.

A conveyancer acting for a buyer should seek confirmation in the pre-contract enquiries that this certificate will be handed over on completion. |
| **C: Charges Register** | This is the third register which contains details of all the negative things affecting the land, often called the 'burdens'. The most common burdens are mortgages and covenants. However, the charges register will give notice of other rights and interests to which the property is subject such as leases and rights-of-way.

Note that not all registers will include a charges register. |
| `1 (02.11.2001) A Conveyance dated 10 May 1985 made between Marcus Franks (1) and Norman Butters (2) contains covenants details of which are `**`contained in the schedule hereto`** | Entry 1 of the charges register was created when the title was first registered and indicates that there are some covenants (that is, obligations) affecting the land. HMLR has taken the covenants from this conveyance and has added them to the register in the schedule which is at the bottom of the charges register.

Note that this conveyance is not available for download. It does not contain the words 'copy filed' (or similar) beneath it. HMLR has included everything of relevance in this conveyance on the register itself. |
| `2 (02.11.2001) a Conveyance of the land in this title dated 15 November 1942` | Entry 2 of the charges register indicates that there is a conveyance dated 15 November 1942 which contains covenants affecting the land. However, note that the conveyance was not produced to HMLR when the title was first registered. |

made between Laurie Trims (1) and Peter Yardley (2) contains covenants. **Neither the original conveyance nor a certified copy or an examined abstract was produced on first registration**	The conveyancer acting for the buyer must raise a pre-contract enquiry requesting that the seller provides undisclosed covenants indemnity insurance on completion (see Chapter 5). The seller's conveyancer might advise their client not to meet the cost of this insurance. Ultimately, it is a matter for negotiation between the parties and the buyer's conveyancer may conclude that their buyer client should pay for the indemnity insurance, particularly if there is a lender involved.
3 (02.11.2001) A Conveyance dated 19 March 1989 made between Butters Builders Limited (1) and Amy Newbold (2) contains covenants. *NOTE: Copy filed*	Entry 3 of the charges register indicates that there is a conveyance dated 19 March 1989 which contains covenants. You will note that this entry has the words 'copy filed' beneath it. This means that the document is available for download and should be supplied by the seller's conveyancer as part of the pre-contract package. The buyer's conveyancer should raise a pre-contract enquiry asking for the conveyance is it is not included in the contract pack. You will note that HMLR has not included the details contained in this document in a schedule on the register. Where matters contained in a deed are lengthy, normally HMLR does not set out the full details in the register. This enables HMLR to process applications more quickly and matters contained in a document are sometimes best understood when read with the rest of the deed.
4 (18.01.2017) REGISTERED CHARGE dated **10 January 2017** to	Entries 3 and 4 were added to the register at the time of Sophia's purchase and relate to a mortgage in favour of National Westminster Bank plc. You will see that the registered charge is

secure the moneys including the further advances therein mentioned. 5 (18.01.2017) PROPRIETOR: National Westminster Bank plc (Co Regn No 929027) of Mortgage Centre, PO Box 123, Greenock PA15 1EF	dated with the same date as appears at entry 4 of the proprietorship register. Note that the charges register contains details of registered mortgages and notice of other financial burdens secured on the property but does not give details of the amount of money involved.
THE SCHEDULE ABOVE REFERRED TO 1. Not to use the property as anything other than a single residential dwelling without the written consent of the Vendor or his successors in title. 2. Not to do or cause anything to be done on the property which may be or become a nuisance or	You will remember from entry 1 of the charges register that the conveyance dated 10 May 1985 contains covenants and that these were included in the schedule on the charges register. Covenant 1 prohibits the property from being used as anything other than a residential dwelling (without the consent of the original seller in 1985 or their successors in title). Covenant 2 is a fairly general obligation which provides that the registered proprietor must not do anything which becomes a nuisance or annoyance to neighbouring properties. From a buyer's point of view, neither of these covenants are of particular concern unless School House has been used as more than one dwelling already or if a buyer wants to use the land as more than one dwelling. An example might be building an additional dwelling on the land.

annoyance to the neighbouring properties.	
END OF REGISTER	Always look for this wording as it indicates the end of the register.
Title plan	We have not produced the title plan for School House but remember that every register will have an accompanying title plan registered under the same title number. The extent of the property falling within the title will be edged red on the title plan.

In most cases, conveyancers will obtain copies of the registers of title and any associated documents using the electronic HMLR portal. However, it is possible to use forms. From OC1 will be used to obtain official copies of a register and the associated title plan. Form OC2 will be used to obtain official copies of documents only.

For more information about the HMLR portal, follow this link:

https://www.gov.uk/government/collections/how-to-use-the-land-registry-portal

Land law links

You can hopefully see how the land law which you considered in Chapter 1 comes to life when thinking about the title to a property.

You will see that the property register indicates whether the title relates to freehold or leasehold – you will remember that these are the two legal estates that exist in land.

You will recall that an easement is the right of one landowner over the land of another. If a property benefits from an easement, this will appear on the property register. If a property is burdened by an easement (that is, another landowner can exercise a right over the land within this title), this will appear on the charges register.

A mortgage is an agreement between a borrower and lender to secure a loan. Most people purchasing a residential property will do so with the aid of a mortgage. The mortgage lender thus has an interest which must be protected and this is done by putting a notice of the mortgage on the charges register.

A covenant is a promise to do or not to do something. If a property is burdened by a covenant, this will appear on the charges register. You will see that often, a covenant limits what the property owner can do with the property. You will also appreciate that this it is very important for a buyer to be fully advised by their conveyancer as to the nature of the covenants affecting the land.

You have also seen reference in a register to a conveyance. This is the unregistered land equivalent of a transfer and is the document by which a seller transferred the title to the buyer in exchange for money. Note that a conveyance is an example of a deed.

Practice Points

A register of title which is downloaded from HMLR is called an 'official copy'. The LRA 2002 introduced this term. Prior to the introduction of the act in October 2003, a copy of the register provided by HMLR was called an 'office copy'. It seems like a minor point but, technically, 'office copies' no longer exist. Accordingly, if a firm or conveyancer still uses this term, they should stop doing so. The correct term is 'official copy' and has been since 2003! Similarly, the 'filed plan' no longer exists – it is called a 'title plan'.

Notices and restrictions

We have seen that there are two legal estates in land, freehold and leasehold. This Practical Guide is concerned with the freehold estate. We have also seen that the main characteristic of the freehold estate is the fact that the party with a freehold title can use the land for an unlimited duration (as contrasted with the leasehold estate where the right to use the land will come to an end). However, we have also seen that the rights of the freehold owner can be fettered by rights and interests that other parties have over the land. There may be an easement over the land giving an adjoining landowner a right-of-way. The owner may have purchased the land with the aid of a mortgage. An adjoining landowner might have the benefit of a covenant against building on the land. All of these are examples of 'third-party rights' that is, the rights of parties other than the landowner over the land.

The rights of third parties over land must be protected. The way that these rights are protected in the unregistered system are beyond the scope of this Practical Guide and even in a registered context, the law and practice can be complex. However, in outline, the right of a third-party over land which is registered can be protected in one of two ways:

1   a notice on the register of title; or
2   a restriction on the register of title

You will recall that we have seen examples of some of the most common restrictions, although there are a significant number of them. They are contained in HMLR PG19.

A notice is an entry made in the register in respect of the burden of an interest affecting a registered estate or charge. A restriction is an entry in the register that prevents or regulates the making of an entry in the register in respect of any disposition. The word 'disposition' is not defined in the LRA 2002 or the LRR 2003, but generally describes a transaction which must be completed by registration such as a sale or the grant of a mortgage.

In our fictitious register of title above, all of the entries on the charges register are examples of a notice.

An interest under a trust of land (see Chapter 1), cannot be protected by notice (s33(a)(i) LRA 2002). If someone has a behind-the-scenes beneficial interest in land, for example, this must be protected by the entry of a restriction on the proprietorship register. We have seen that this is done by registering a Form A restriction.

There are specific procedures and forms which must be used to register notices or restrictions. However, in a straightforward residential conveyancing transaction, it is not necessary to make a separate application to register or remove any relevant notices or restrictions as this will be done as part of the registration application made by the buyer's conveyancer after completion (see Chapter 8).

Practice Points

As the name implies, a restriction on a register prohibits the making of an entry in respect of a disposition until such time as the terms of the restriction are complied with. This could mean that someone's consent to the registration is required or that a certificate is required, as in the example of the Form LL restriction at entry 6 of the proprietorship register in our fictitious register above. Thus, a restriction is a danger for a buyer's conveyancer. A restriction could mean that the buyer's registration cannot be concluded after completion of the buyer's purchase. A conveyancer should always look very carefully at the terms of a restriction and, if necessary, raise a pre-contract enquiry. It is essential for a buyer's conveyancer to be satisfied, prior to exchange of contracts, that a restriction can be complied with after completion or that the conveyancer can obtain the necessary consent or certificate after completion. Never assume that it will be straightforward to deal with a restriction once completion has taken place.

The detail of HMLR's practice in relation to notices and restrictions is contained in HMLR PG19.

Overriding interests

We cannot move on from the register of title without a brief mention of overriding interests. This is a class of interests that was created by the LRA 1925 and retained (albeit amended somewhat) in the LRA 2002. An overriding interest is an interest which is capable of binding a buyer (or a mortgagee) despite the fact that it does not appear on the register of title. The whole ethos of the system of land registration is to ensure that, at any point in time, the register gives as complete a picture as possible of the ownership of land and the third-party rights that affect it. You can therefore see that an overriding interest seems completely contradictory to this principle. It is for this reason that overriding interests have been described as a 'blot on the system of land registration'.

There are a number of overriding interests specified in the LRA 2002, but generally the one of most risk and concern to a buyer in a residential conveyancing transaction is the person who is in actual occupation of the property who has an interest in the land but, crucially, does not appear on the register of title.

This means that if someone lives at a property (that is, they have actual occupation) and, for example, has contributed towards the purchase price (which is what given them 'rights' in the land), they may have an overriding interest. The significance of this is that their interest can bind a buyer, even though they do not appear on the register of title.

There is a distinction between registered and unregistered land in relation to such rights. Note, however, that the term 'overriding interest' only applies to registered land. Whether a buyer is bound by an overriding interest will, broadly, depend on whether inquiry has been made of the occupier who does not appear on the register of title.

Practice Points

So how does a buyer's conveyancer guard against the risk of a buyer being bound by the interest of a person who does not appear on the register of title?

The answer to this question demonstrates the importance of the 'conveyancing jigsaw' that we mentioned at the outset. Some of the steps that we take in the conveyancing transaction only make sense when we look at big picture.

As you will see, the Property Information Form is completed by the seller and forms part of the contract package. Question 11 of this form deals with occupiers at the seller's property. It asks whether the seller lives at the property and whether anyone else aged over 17 lives there. The question goes on to ask the full names of any occupiers and to specify whether any of them are tenants or lodgers.

This will tell the buyer's conveyancer about any non-owning occupiers, for example, an adult child living with their parents or an elderly parent living in a 'granny annexe'.

The buyer's conveyancer will advise their buyer to carry out a physical inspection of the property as part of the pre-contract searches and enquiries. This means that the buyer must re-visit the property and look for evidence of occupiers.

The Property Information Form also asks the seller to confirm that any occupier over the age of 17 will agree to leave the property on completion and sign the contract. As we will see, the contract incorporating the

Standard Conditions of Sale (5th edition – 2018 revision) contains pre-printed special condition 7 to deal with this point.

So, all of the above pieces of the jigsaw must come together firstly to assist a buyer's conveyancer to identify whether there is a non-owning occupier and secondly to ensure that appropriate steps are taken to secure vacant possession on completion. If the buyer's conveyancer is in any doubt, they should advise their buyer not to exchange contracts until the position relating to a non-owning occupier is resolved.

And a brief word on the position of the seller's conveyancer. Remember that the seller will be the conveyancer's client. A non-owning occupier may have a claim against the sale proceeds of the property. This could give rise to a conflict-of-interest between the seller and the occupier and, at the very least, raises a *significant risk* of a conflict. Accordingly, the seller's conveyancer should not also act for the occupier. They should send the contract to the occupier for signature and return but also tell the occupier to obtain their own independent legal advice if they are in any doubt as to their position.

CHAPTER FIVE

TAKING INSTRUCTIONS AND INDEMNITY INSURANCE

The fact that we are at Chapter 5 and have still not started to talk in detail about the conveyancing process itself tells you a lot about the 'frontloading' of all of the due diligence and checks that we must make at the beginning of every conveyancing file. This Chapter considers the start of the conveyancing process on a residential freehold sale and purchase when we take instructions from our clients and the information that we should obtain. This Chapter will conclude with a brief discussion about indemnity insurance.

Stage of the conveyancing process

SELLER	BUYER
MARKETING STAGE OF THE TRANSACTION	
Markets property with an estate agent Obtains Energy Performance Certificate Sale agreed Conveyancer is instructed	Views property Makes offer to buy property Agrees price via estate agent Conveyancer is instructed
PRE-EXCHANGE STAGE OF THE TRANSACTION	
Conveyancer takes instructions from client: • Identification / due diligence / AML • Client care letter	Conveyancer takes instructions from client: • Identification / due diligence / AML • Client care letter

Recap

You will recall that in earlier Chapters we have considered the due diligence and regulatory issues which are imposed on conveyancers including:

- identification checks
- AML requirements
- source of funds and source of wealth checks
- the contents of the client care letter

Every firm will deal with the conveyancing process in a slightly different way. Some will deal with all of the above points prior to creating the retainer and taking detailed instructions from their client. Others might take instructions before concluding all due diligence. We will now move on to look at the information which a conveyancer should obtain from their client at the outset of a sale and purchase. This information gathering exercise is essential to ensure that the conveyancer properly understands their client's requirements and makes no incorrect assumptions. If the conveyancer gets anything wrong, they could face a negligence claim from the client (that is a claim for any losses incurred by the client as a result of poor advice).

Note that throughout this Practical Guide we will always consider the sale transaction before the purchase.

Taking instructions on a sale

Conveyancers must take full instructions from the seller to ensure that they have the complete picture as to their clients' circumstances and priorities. As we have seen, it is essential to ensure that a conveyancer does not make any assumptions about their client. We will look at the information that a conveyancer needs to obtain in most residential freehold sale transactions. This is likely to be done at a similar time to when all of the identification and due diligence requirements is obtained.

The seller's conveyancer must be satisfied that the seller has good title to the property and is entitled to sell it. This means that the seller's conveyancer must investigate the seller's title as we saw in Chapter 4. As we will see in Chapter 6, the seller's conveyancer will draft the contract of sale.

Practice Points

As a matter of professional conduct, a conveyancer must ensure that they take instructions from all sellers of a property. This means engaging with and taking direct instructions from all sellers rather than simply relying on the word of one seller. Some firms insist on seeing all clients at a face-to-face meeting (or an online meeting) to take these instructions.

Typical instruction checklist

Below is a checklist of information and why it is needed.

Information	Why it is needed
Full name, address and contact details of all sellers	To contact the seller To ensure that identification documents are obtained To cross check with the title in readiness for drafting the contract
Address of property to be sold	This is often the property that the seller is living in but it is important to make no assumptions
Name and address of estate agent, if relevant	Most sellers will market and sell a property using an estate agent who will send details of the transaction in their memorandum of sale when a buyer is found If an estate agent is not used, an agreement reached directly between the seller and buyer is called a 'private sale'
Has an Energy Performance Certificate been obtained?	The estate agent will usually provide the EPC It is a legal requirement that the seller makes an EPC available to a buyer The seller might use the EPC from when they purchased the property – they are valid for 10 years

	The estate agent should provide a copy of the EPC with the memorandum of sale (or a link to it)
	Link: https://www.gov.uk/find-energy-certificate
Agreed sale price of property	This figure will be inserted in the contract
Has an additional sum be agreed with the buyer for any Fittings and Contents?	If the buyer agrees to purchase any additional items from the seller, the figure should be inserted in the contract and a list of the items included as an extra special condition
	At this relatively early stage, the seller and buyer are unlikely to have negotiated a price for additional items – this will often happen once the buyer's conveyancer receives the contract pack which includes the Fittings and Contents Form (see Chapter 6)
Name and address, if known, of all buyers	The details of the buyers must be inserted in the contract
	Often the seller does not have this information and it will be provided by the estate agent on the memorandum of sale
	It is important to carry out a conflict check when full details are known
Name and address, if known, of buyer's conveyancer	Often the seller does not have this information and it will be provided by the estate agent on the memorandum of sale
Is the property to be sold freehold or leasehold?	This must be inserted in the contract and the tenure should be cross checked with the title
Details regarding title to the property	In most cases, the title to the property will be registered at HMLR
	Often the seller does not know the title number to the property – this will not matter as the conveyancer can obtain it (see Chapter 6)

Does the seller currently live in property to be sold?	This is important If the seller does not live there, the conveyancer must establish whether the property is currently empty (vacant) or whether someone else lives in the property The seller's conveyancer must also be satisfied that the seller is the true owner of the property. If the seller does not live in the property to be sold, we have seen that best practice demands that the conveyancer obtains documentary evidence linking the seller to the property being sold
Has the seller lived in the property throughout their entire ownership of the property?	This is relevant to the seller's taxation position If a seller has not lived in a property for the entire period of their ownership, they may be liable to pay Capital Gains Tax (CGT) on the sale proceeds on completion Note that most sellers do not have to worry about the possibility of paying CGT when they sell a property due to the private residence relief. Even if a substantial gain has been made between the purchase of the property and its eventual sale, if the property has been the seller's home, no CGT will be payable *Practice Points* This is not something which a conveyancer should advise about in detail because we are lawyers not accountants. However, the conveyancer should advise the seller to obtain detailed accountancy advice prior to exchange of contracts if there is a possibility that CGT might be payable on the sale proceeds. Note that the report of the sale and any CGT payable must be submitted to HMRC within 60 days of completion, which is a relatively new and very tight timeframe
Does anyone other than the seller who is over the age of 17 live at the property with the seller?	We have seen that a non-owning occupier can cause a problem for a buyer. The buyer's conveyancer will want to ensure that overreaching takes place, if relevant, and that any non-owning occupier signs the contract as evidence of their

	intention to move out of the property on completion The seller must declare who lives in the property at question 11 of the Property Information Form but it is helpful for the seller's conveyancer to obtain this information at the beginning of the transaction
If the property is tenanted, the seller must provide full details of the tenants, the tenancy agreement, any money held in the Tenant Deposit Scheme and any managing agent	If the property is going to be sold with a tenant living in it, the seller's conveyancer must ensure that the contract is properly drafted (see Chapter 6, and, in particular, special condition 4 of the contract). In most cases, the seller will contract with the buyer to handover an empty property on completion. This is known as giving 'vacant possession'. However, if the seller is selling with a tenant in (which makes it a buy to let transaction), the contract must be accurately drafted to reflect this
What is the current use of the property?	In most cases, the use of the property will be residential However, it is important for the seller's conveyancer to understand whether, for example, there has been any business use at property as this is another circumstance where CGT might be payable on the sale proceeds
Has the seller carried out any work to the property?	This information should be included on the Property Information Form but if the seller has installed new windows, for example, or built an extension, the conveyancer must ensure that the seller produces the correct documentation
Are there any issues of interest or concern regarding the location of the property?	For example, the property might be near a public footpath or a river – the seller's conveyancer should point out that the buyer's conveyancer will probably do additional searches and raise additional enquiries in this regard (see Chapter 7)

Is the property in mortgage?	This is an essential question The seller's conveyancer will be required to give an undertaking to redeem (pay off) all mortgages appearing on the seller's charges register (see Chapter 4) so it is essential for the seller's conveyancer to fully understand at this early stage of the transaction whether there are any registered charges
Ask the seller to provide details of the lender, address and the mortgage account number, if relevant	The seller's conveyancer will check the charges register of the title to establish whether the seller has any registered charges over the property *Practice Points* An essential part of the risk management process for the seller's conveyancer is to write to all lenders to obtain indicative redemption figures on all registered charges prior to exchange of contracts. This is to ensure that the sale price is sufficient to pay off the mortgage/s on completion
Are there any other loans secured on the property?	The seller may have other loans secured against the property in addition to mortgages. The seller's conveyancer must have details of all of them to ensure that there are sufficient sale proceeds to pay off all charges registered over the property
Is the seller in arrears with any mortgages or secured loans?	The possibility of arrears on a mortgage or secured loan may mean that another law firm has been instructed to start possession proceedings against the seller *Practice Points* If possession proceedings have been started against the seller this makes it a much riskier and more difficult transaction. An inexperienced conveyancer should immediately pass the file to a qualified colleague if they discover that the seller is having difficulties paying their existing mortgage
Has the seller had any correspondence with a lender about arrears?	The seller should be asked to provide copies of any correspondence that they have had with their lender particularly in relation to arrears or possession proceedings – see above

Some firms may also ask whether the seller has any loans or borrowing connected with a business which they run	The reason for asking this is that sometimes, business borrowing can be tied in with a person's home. This can mean that in addition to any money owing on a residential mortgage secured on the property, the lender may also want the business borrowing to be paid out of the sale proceeds on completion
Ask seller for details of bank account to which the net sale proceeds are to be sent	The money that is left over on a sale after all mortgages, legal fees and other expenses (for example, estate agent's fees) have been paid is called the 'net sale proceeds' If the seller has a related purchase transaction, it is likely that the net sale proceeds will be transferred to the purchase file However, if the seller wants the sale proceeds to be sent to a bank account, the conveyancer will usually ask for details of the bank account to which the sale proceeds are to be sent at an early stage in the transaction. This will usually be a UK based bank account in the name of the seller
Is the sale dependent on a related purchase transaction?	This is an essential question In most cases, the seller will instruct the same conveyancer to act on their related sale and purchase
Is the seller willing to proceed on their sale independently of their purchase?	Most sellers want to move from one house to the other on the same day – this is known as synchronising the transactions It can be helpful to know at the beginning of a transaction whether will not seller could go ahead on their sale independently of their purchase transaction. This would mean moving out of the house they are living in now, storing their furniture and having someone else to live prior to their purchase transaction going ahead As we will see, if the sale transaction proceeds more quickly than the purchase, the seller's conveyancer will need to obtain their client's irrevocable authority to go ahead on the sale independently of the purchase at the time of exchange of contracts

Are there any particular requirements regarding a proposed completion date or dates to avoid?	The Protocol requires the parties to indicate whether they have a target completion date and communicate this beginning of the transaction It can be helpful to know whether the seller is going on holiday, for example and whether there are any dates to avoid
Consider asking all sellers to sign and return the checklist or provide their signature in some other way	Obtaining the seller's signatures is an important part of the due diligence and identification processes Ideally, the conveyancer will see the seller face to face and will ask them to sign the completed checklist. This gives an up-to-date signature which can be cross checked with the seller's identification documents
The seller's conveyancer might check whether they acted on the purchase of the property for the seller	If so, the seller's conveyancer will obtain the old purchase file from storage as it may contain information which is helpful for the sale
The conveyancer might ask: Are you aware of any bankruptcy proceedings being issued against you or anyone involved with your sale? If so, please provide details.	If a seller is aware of pending bankruptcy proceedings, it is unlikely that they will be able to proceed with the sale and the conveyancer must be cautious If the sale is going to proceed, it would probably need to involve a trustee in bankruptcy
The conveyancer might ask: Is there any other information which you think would be useful to us in relation to your sale?	Clients often fail to give the conveyancer all relevant information about their transaction. Whilst this question can seem a bit open-ended, it might elicit additional information that is relevant
The conveyancer might ask:	This is a general request from the conveyancer for permission to deal with people who are likely to crop up during the transaction. The reason for

Please confirm that we may discuss details of your sale/purchase/ mortgage with your estate agent/lender/ mortgage broker (as appropriate)	asking this information is to avoid problems with confidentiality
Hopefully you can see that much of the information that is taken from the seller at this early-stage helps with the Know Your Client process	

Taking instructions on a purchase

Conveyancers must take full instructions from the buyer to ensure that they have the complete picture as to their clients' circumstances and priorities. As we have seen, it is essential to ensure that a conveyancer does not make any assumptions about their client. We will look at the information that a conveyancer needs to obtain in most residential freehold purchase transactions. This is likely to be done at a similar time to all of the identification and due diligence requirements is obtained.

Practice Points

As a matter of professional conduct, a conveyancer must ensure that they take instructions from all buyers of a property. This means engaging with and taking direct instructions from all buyers rather than simply relying on the word of one buyer. Some firms insist on seeing all clients at a face-to-face meeting (or an online meeting) to take these instructions.

Typical instruction checklist

Below is a checklist of information and why it is needed.

Information	Why it is needed
Full name, address and contact details of all buyers	To contact the buyer To ensure that identification documents are obtained To obtain full name to insert into the contract
Address of property to be purchased	To ensure the contract is properly drafted and searches are carried out against the correct property
Name and address of estate agent, if relevant	Most sellers will market and sell a property using an estate agent who will send details of the transaction in their memorandum of sale when a buyer is found
Has an Energy Performance Certificate been obtained?	The estate agent will usually provide the EPC It is a legal requirement that the seller makes an EPC available to a buyer The seller might use the EPC from when they purchased the property – they are valid for 10 years The estate agent should provide a copy of the EPC with the memorandum of sale (or a link to it) Link: https://www.gov.uk/find-energy-certificate The buyer's conveyancer should ensure that their client receives a copy of the EPC and that it is valid
Agreed purchase price of property	This figure will be inserted in the contract (and transfer) and should appear in the mortgage offer if a mortgage is needed
Has an additional sum be agreed with the seller for any Fittings and Contents?	If the buyer agrees to purchase any additional items from the seller, the figure should be inserted in the contract and a list of the items included as an extra special condition

	At this relatively early stage, the seller and buyer are unlikely to have negotiated a price for additional items – this will often happen once the buyer's conveyancer receives the contract pack which includes the Fittings and Contents Form (see Chapter 6)
Name and address, if known, of all sellers	Often the buyer does not have this information and it will be provided by the estate agent on the memorandum of sale Important to carry out a conflict check when full details are known
Name and address, if known, of seller's conveyancer	Often the buyer does not have this information and it will be provided by the estate agent on the memorandum of sale
Is the property to be sold freehold or leasehold?	This must be inserted in the contract and the tenure should be cross checked with the title
If the property is tenanted, the seller must provide full details of the tenants, the tenancy agreement, any money held in the Tenant Deposit Scheme and any managing agent	If the property is going to be sold with a tenant living in it, the buyer's conveyancer must ensure that the contract is properly drafted (see Chapter 6, and, in particular, special condition 4 of the contract). In most cases, the seller will contract with the buyer to handover an empty property on completion. This is known as giving 'vacant possession'. However, if the seller is selling with a tenant in (which makes it a buy to let transaction), the contract must be accurately drafted to reflect this
What is the current use of the property?	In most cases, the use of the property will be residential
What is the buyer's proposed use of the property?	In most cases, the buyer is purchasing the property to live in but if the buyer intends to use it for a different purpose, the conveyancer must check the use and title of the property and consider whether there are any planning implications

Does the buyer propose making any changes/alterations to the property?	The conveyancer must check the title of the property and consider whether there are any planning implications
Are there any issues of interest or concern regarding the location of the property?	For example, the property might be near a public footpath or a river – the buyer's conveyancer will probably do additional searches and raise additional enquiries in this regard (see Chapter 7)
How will the purchase be funded?	This is an essential question Even if the buyer has a related sale and/or needs a mortgage, they are likely to be contributing some of their own money to the purchase We have seen in Chapter 3 the importance of source of funds and source of wealth checks from the point of view of AML and Lender's Handbook requirements
Is there a gifted deposit?	As we have seen, it is very common for a relation to contribute towards the purchase of a property This information must be obtained from the buyer and the issues discussed in Chapter 3 regarding source of funds and source of wealth and avoiding conflicts of interest must all be considered
If a mortgage is required, ask the buyer to provide details of the mortgage broker (if any), lender and amount to be borrowed	This is part of the due diligence but the buyer's conveyancer will also need to check whether their firm is able to act for the lender as well in the transaction. To do so, the firm must be on the 'panel' of firms that the lender is willing to use
Is the purchase dependent on a related sale transaction?	This is an essential question In most cases, the buyer will instruct the same conveyancer to act on their related sale and purchase

Are there any particular requirements regarding a proposed completion date or dates to avoid?	The Protocol requires the parties to indicate whether they have a target completion date and communicate this beginning of the transaction
	It can be helpful to know whether the buyer is going on holiday, for example and whether there are any dates to avoid
Consider asking all buyers to sign and return the checklist or provide their signature in some other way	Obtaining the buyer's signatures is an important part of the due diligence and identification processes
	Ideally, the conveyancer will see the buyer face to face and will ask them to sign the completed checklist. This gives an up-to-date signature which can be cross checked with the buyer's identification documents
Stamp Duty Land Tax (SDLT)	The conveyancer must obtain enough information to give an estimate in the client care letter of the amount of SDLT payable on completion (see Chapter 8)
	A CQS accredited firm must have a policy in place to enable the firm to track and cross check SDLT figures given throughout a transaction
	If the property is in Wales, Land Transaction Tax (LTT) will be payable
Ask the buyer to provide information required to submit the SDLT application on completion	An answer to one of the following must be provided:
	National Insurance number and date of birth (box 49 on SDLT form)
	VAT registration number (box 50)
	Company or partnership Unique Transaction Reference (UTR) (box 51)

The conveyancer might ask: Are you aware of any bankruptcy proceedings being issued against you or anyone involved with your purchase? If so, please provide details.	If a buyer is aware of bankruptcy proceedings, it is unlikely that the transaction will go ahead particularly if a mortgage is required *Practice Points* Many conveyancers will carry out a bankruptcy search against their buyer client at the beginning of the transaction to check for any bankruptcy proceedings Note that this search will be repeated before completion if the buyer is funding the purchase with the aid of a mortgage (see Chapter 8)
The conveyancer might ask: Is there any other information which you think would be useful to us in relation to your purchase?	Clients often fail to give the conveyancer all relevant information about their transaction. Whilst this question can seem a bit open-ended, it might elicit additional information that is relevant
The conveyancer might ask: Please confirm that we may discuss details of your sale/purchase/mortgage with your estate agent/lender/mortgage broker (as appropriate)	This is a general request from the conveyancer for permission to deal with people who are likely to crop up during the transaction. The reason for asking this information is to avoid problems with confidentiality
Hopefully you can see that much of the information that is taken from the buyer at this early-stage helps with the Know Your Client process	

Indemnity insurance

It might seem odd to deal with a topic that is likely to arise during a transaction in the same chapter as taking instructions. However, indemnity insurance is frequently seen as a 'solution' by conveyancers acting on a sale or purchase to a problem which may arise. It is important to understand from the outset that indemnity insurance is hardly ever a 'solution' in that it does not put the technical, legal problem which has arisen right. Rather, indemnity insurance is often a cheap route around a problem, thus enabling a transaction to proceed.

Practice Points

There are significant limitations in relation to indemnity insurance one of the most important of which being that no enquiry must be made of any person or organisation in the event that a problem arises. For example, if a property does not enjoy the benefit of a legal right-of-way (easement) to it from the public highway, and the seller's conveyancer contacts the owner of the intervening land, it will almost invariably not be possible to obtain indemnity insurance and the transaction might fall through. Accordingly, all conveyancers must understand that they should not make contact with anyone in the event that indemnity insurance might be needed. Furthermore, they should advise their clients not to make any such contact.

What is indemnity insurance?

On the sale of a property, defects might be discovered that are not capable of swift remedy or remedy at all. A conveyancer may decide that a defective title indemnity policy is required to enable the transaction to proceed. Indemnity insurance protects the buyer and lender against financial loss that could result from the relevant defects. Many legal defects arising in a conveyancing transaction can be insured in this way.

Usually, the insurance gives the parties a reasonably priced, prompt way of enabling the transaction to proceed whilst protecting the buyer (and lender, if any).

If a problem is discovered for which an indemnity insurance policy might be a suitable solution, the conveyancers for the seller and buyer must explain the situation and implications to their respective clients and discuss the cost of the policy with their client.

Practice Points

It is the seller's responsibility to provide a good title to the buyer. Accordingly, the seller would be expected to pay for an indemnity policy and reference should be made to the provision of the policy in the contract on exchange. Ideally, a copy of the required indemnity insurance policy should be attached to the contract. In addition, if the seller is required to swear a statutory declaration or provide a statement of truth as to facts (for example, as to the route of a right-of-way and its use), this should also be attached to the contract for the sake of clarity.

However, the seller's conveyancer will often advise the client not to pay for indemnity insurance. This might be because the defect is very old and unlikely to be a problem. In this case, the buyer's conveyancer should consider advising their client to pay for the required indemnity insurance particularly if they have a lender involved. Ultimately, if the buyer's conveyancer considers that an indemnity policy is required, it will be a matter for negotiation between the parties as to who pays for it.

Just a note about terminology. Do not confuse reference to indemnity insurance policies in this Chapter with reference to 'professional indemnity insurance' in Chapter 2. The latter is the insurance which law firms must have in place as a regulatory requirement to compensate clients in the event that they suffer loss due to some fault of the law firm.

When is an indemnity insurance policy needed?

If a defect is discovered, the conveyancer must use their professional judgement to decide whether the defect can be remedied. In many cases, it might be possible to remedy a legal defect but it would probably take too much time and money to resolve. Accordingly, in many cases the conveyancer will conclude that an indemnity insurance policy is a suitable way to proceed. The ultimate decision rests with the conveyancer based on their assessment of the risk involved.

There is a wide range of indemnity insurance policies available from a number of providers. However, examples of situations where indemnity insurance is obtained are:

- a failure to obtain planning permission for building work to a property
- a failure to obtain building regulation consent for work which is being carried out the property
- if a property falls in an area that is at risk of chancel liability (see Chapter 7)
- no documentation relating to the installation of windows at a property (for example, Fensa certificates)

Land law links

In addition to the above, you will notice that indemnity insurance is often sought in the event that there is legal problem with the title. Examples of the sort of issues that you will come across in your land law are:

- lack of easement – for example, a property does not enjoy a right of access or to a right to use pipes, sewers and cables
- breach of a restrictive covenant – for example, there is a covenant on the title which provides that only one dwelling should be built on the plot of land but someone has built an additional property
- covenants which are referred to on the title but the document containing them is not available (see register of title in Chapter 4) – these are known as 'undisclosed covenants'

As indicated above, it is important to realise that the indemnity insurance does not put the technical legal problem right. The way to resolve a lack of a right-of-way is a legal deed of easement between the owner of the property over which the right-of-way is required and the owner of the property which needs the right-of-way. This can be time-consuming and expensive to produce and, of course, the property owners might not be able to come to an agreement.

If consent to do something is required under the terms of a covenant, the way to comply with the covenant is to obtain written consent from the party entitled to give it. This can also be difficult to achieve particularly if it is not possible to identify who has the benefit of the covenant. If indemnity insurance is sought to deal with these issues, it is important to understand that the insurance does not correct the legal defect. It does not magically produce the required deed of easement or covenant consent. The indemnity insurance simply provides protection in that it provides a financial remedy in the event that someone tries to enforce a legal right.

The indemnity insurance policy

Generally, the policy is a single premium policy meaning that a 'one off' payment is required. This is usually paid on completion. The policy should protect the buyer, their successors in title (that is, subsequent owners) and any lender.

Many indemnity insurance policies are available 'off-the-shelf' meaning that the insurer does not need to receive details of the particular property or the particular problem. The conveyancer will often apply for a standard policy online. Conveyancers might obtain quotations from 2 or 3 indemnity insurance providers or the search company which the firm uses might offer this facility.

In some cases, and off-the-shelf policy will not suffice. In this case, the indemnity insurer will need to assess the risk and will need:

- the precise nature of the defect
- a copy of any document in which the defect appears (if relevant)
- the date the defect or problem arose
- whether any steps have been taken to remedy the defect
- whether any third parties have been informed or involved
- an estimate of the amount of cover required (typically the amount of the purchase price)

The indemnity insurer will then provide a draft policy for consideration by the conveyancer.

Practice Points

An inexperienced conveyancer will not necessarily be able to assess the risk of when and indemnity insurance policy might be acceptable. All of the above defects involve a number of variables for example how recently a covenant was imposed or building work was carried out. The more recent the defect, the more expensive and indemnity insurance policy is likely to be, if one is available at all.

If indemnity insurance is considered to be an acceptable solution, it is also essential to ensure that the proposed indemnity insurance policy covers the required defect and protects both the buyer and lender, if any. The policy should also not have any exclusions which might make it worthless to the buyer.

The most important risk management requirements are that a conveyancer does not accept indemnity insurance on a purchase if they are unsure as to the terms of policy. If there is a lender involved, it may also be necessary to check the Lender's Handbook (section 9) to establish whether the lender will accept indemnity insurance in the particular situation. It is also essential to ensure that no third-party is contacted who might have some interest in the issue. For example:

- do not contact the planning or building regulation departments of the local authority if these documents have not been obtained
- do not contact an adjoining landowner if they have the benefit of covenant which has been breached
- do not contact an adjoining landowner over which a right of access is exercised

CHAPTER SIX
PROGRESSING A SALE
TRANSACTION

Once a conveyancer has taken instructions from their seller client, the onus is now on the conveyancer to prepare the draft contract pack. Generally, a transaction will only proceed in a meaningful way once the contract pack has been issued to the buyer's conveyancer. In this Chapter, we will look at the steps to be taken to produce the contract pack and how a straightforward contract for a residential freehold property is drafted. We will not repeat detailed content that has been covered elsewhere in this Practical Guide.

Stage of the conveyancing process

SELLER	BUYER
PRE-EXCHANGE STAGE OF THE TRANSACTION	
Obtain seller's title Ask seller to complete Protocol forms	
Draft sale contract	
Send contract package to buyer's conveyancer: • Contract in duplicate • Seller's title • Protocol forms • Any guarantees, planning permissions etc	

Contents of the contract pack

The contract pack will contain the following basic information and documents:

- the draft contract in duplicate. It is sent to the buyer's conveyancer in duplicate to enable the buyer's conveyancer to insert their client's name and address and make any other amendments. They will return one copy of the contract to the seller's conveyancer and each conveyancer will arrange for their client to sign in readiness for exchange

- the Protocol forms

- the seller's title

- any documents that will be relevant to a buyer, such as planning permissions or guarantees (for example, for boilers or windows)

Practice Points

Many firms will submit the contract pack to the buyer's conveyancer in hardcopy by post or document exchange. An increasing number, however, will submit the contract pack by email. The Protocol permits the contract bundle to be sent by email but requires the seller's conveyancer to inform the buyers conveyancer of this intention and, importantly, to ensure that each document is a separately identifiable attachment or is uploaded individually (para 13).

The seller's conveyancer should send the plan of the property to their seller client prior to drafting the contract to seek the seller's confirmation that the plan is correct and represents the full extent of the property being sold.

Work required to prepare the contract pack

Obtain the seller's title

We have seen that this is likely to involve downloading the register entries, title plan and any documents referred to in the registers from the HMLR portal. HMLR's e-business customers can use MapSearch which is a free digital service to establish whether land in England and Wales is registered, view the location of the land and obtain the title number.

If the sellers title is unregistered, the conveyancer must locate the title deeds. If the property is in mortgage, they will be held with a lender. The conveyancer must request the release of the title deeds and give the lender an undertaking confirming that the original documents will not be released to anyone (for example, the buyer's conveyancer) until the mortgage is redeemed.

Protocol forms

The seller will complete a Property Information Form. This is designed to give a buyer practical information about the property. In addition, the seller will complete a Fittings and Contents Form. As the name suggests, this provides a list of the items in the property which will be included in the sale price and those which the seller will be removing. The completed form is attached to the contract on exchange.

Drafting the contract

This is the major task that the seller's conveyancer will carry out once the seller has provided instructions and the conveyancer has obtained their client's title. The contract which is used for the vast majority of residential conveyancing transactions in England and Wales is the Law Society's form of the contract. It is a contract incorporating the Standard Conditions of Sale (5th edition – 2018 revision).

The full version of the contract can be found by following this link:

https://www.lawsociety.org.uk/en/topics/property/standard-conditions-of-sale

We will consider how to draft the contract and will assume that we are acting for Sophia Hayward who is selling School House, The Green, Barnford, Berkshire BR5 6YH, the fictitious register of title for which can be found in Chapter 4. We will assume that Sophia let out the property to a tenant when she first purchased it but when the tenant moved out last year, Sophia moved back into the property with her partner, Andrew Jones. The sale price is £525,000 and the buyer has agreed to pay an additional £2000 for all carpets and curtains. It has been agreed that Sophia will remove a built-in barbecue in the back garden when she moves out. Sophia does not have a related purchase transaction.

Particulars of sale		
This is the front page of the contract and sets out the specifics for the particular transaction in hand		
Content of contract	How it should be drafted	Notes
Date		This is left blank when the contract is drafted. The date of exchange of contracts is hand written in here upon exchange.
Seller	Sophia Carol Hayward of School House, The Green, Barnford, Berkshire BR5 6YH	Note you do not need to put 'Ms' or 'Miss'. Just include the full name as per the proprietorship register. This should tie in with the identification documents which you have required as part of the due diligence process. Include the address that the seller is living at.
Buyer		You have not been given the details of the buyer. This will usually be included on the estate agent's memorandum of sale. However, it is often left blank when the contract is drafted and the buyer's conveyancer will insert their buyer client's full name and address.
Property (freehold/~~leasehold~~)	School House, The Green, Barnford, Berkshire BR5 6YH	Insert the address of the property as it appears on the property register of title. The property register indicates that this is a freehold property so we delete 'leasehold'

Title number/~~root of title~~	SK98765	Insert the title number of the property as it appears on the register. Delete 'root of title' as this is relevant to an unregistered title
Specified encumbrances	All those matters contained or referred to in the charges register of the title (save for financial charges)	This provision indicates the encumbrances, that is, the negative things subject to which property is being sold. You will recall that there are some covenants on the charges register. Different conveyancing firms will have slightly different wording for this provision but note that in all cases, it must be clear that the property is not being sold subject to any financial charges appearing on the charges register. This is because they will be paid off out of the sale proceeds on completion (see Chapter 8).
Title guarantee (full/ ~~limited~~)	Full	The title guarantee is a promise imposed by statute on the seller, which are buyer can rely on after completion. In essence, the seller promises that they have the right to sell the property and that they will, at their own cost, do all that they can to transfer the title to the buyer. A full title guarantee promises that the seller is selling the property free from all

		charges and encumbrances (other than those appearing in the contract). A limited title guarantee is narrower and only warrants that the seller has not created any charges or granted any rights which have not been disclosed. A seller who has lived at the property would give a full title guarantee. A personal representative in a probate sale, for example, would only give a limited title guarantee.
Completion date		This is left blank when the contract is drafted. The date of completion is hand written in here upon exchange.
Contract rate	The Law Society's Rate	The contract rate is the penalty rate of interest that applies in the event of late completion. As an alternative to the Law Society's rate, many conveyancing firms may show this as, for example, '4% above the base rate of [insert major bank] from time to time in force'
Purchase price	£525,000	Insert the agreed purchase price. This will usually be found on the estate agent's memorandum of sale but it is essential to check this with the seller.

Deposit	£ 52,500	A buyer is usually expected to pay a deposit of 10% of the purchase price on exchange of contracts, so insert this figure when the contract is drafted
Contents price (if separate)	£2000	In many cases, the buyer does not agree to purchase any additional items but if they do, it must be inserted in the contract
Balance	£474,500	This final balancing figure might be left blank when the contract is drafted but we have done the calculation for clarity. You will see that the 10% deposit which is paid on exchange is deducted from the purchase price. Then the sum agreed for the contents (£2000) is added to show the final figure due on completion.

Special conditions

These are the conditions which are relevant to this particular transaction. 7 of them are pre-printed and may need amending – see below

1(a) This contract incorporates the Standard Conditions of Sale (Fifth Edition – 2018 – Revision)		There is no need to amend this special condition
(b) The terms used in this contract have the same meaning when used in the Conditions		There is no need to amend this special condition

2 Subject to the terms of this contract and to the Standard Conditions of Sale, the seller is to transfer the property with either title guarantee or limited title guarantee, as specified on the front page		There is no need to amend this special condition
3(a) The sale includes those contents which are indicated on the attached list as in the sale and the buyer is to pay the contents price for them		There is no need to amend this special condition however, this condition emphasises the importance of ensuring that the agreed, signed, Fittings and Contents form is attached to the contract on exchange
3(b) The sale excludes those fixtures which are at property and are indicated on the attached list as from the sale		There is no need to amend this special condition however, this condition emphasises the importance of ensuring that the agreed, signed, Fittings and Contents form is attached to the contract on exchange
4 The property is sold with vacant possession (or) 4 The property is sold subject to the following leases or tenancies:		'Vacant possession' essentially means that the property will be empty on completion. This is an important special condition. In most residential conveyancing transactions, the seller will be moving out of the property. Accordingly, the alternative special condition for will be

		deleted as we have done here.
		However, if the transaction is a buy to let, whereby a buyer is purchasing a property as an investment with a tenant already living up property, then the first alternative will be deleted and the details of the tenancy agreement will be inserted. This is a riskier transaction and a less experienced conveyancer should ensure that they refer to a qualified colleague
5 Conditions 6.1.2 and 6.1.3 shall take effect as if the time specified in them were [ ] rather than 2.00pm		The standard conditions of sale specify that completion must take place by 2pm on the contractually agreed completion date otherwise completion is treated as taking place on the next working day.
		If a seller has a related purchase, the time for completion in special condition 5 will be brought forward to, say, 1pm to ensure that the sale completes before the purchase. In this case, Sophia does not have a related purchase so there is no need to amend this special condition.

6 Representations Neither party can rely on any representation made by the other, unless made in writing by the other or his conveyancer, but this does not exclude liability for fraud or recklessness		There is no need to amend this special condition. It is included to try to ensure that neither party can try to withdraw from the transaction after exchange due to reliance on verbal statements made by the other.
7 Occupier's consent Each occupier identified below agrees with the seller and the buyer, in consideration of their entering into this contract, that the occupier concurs in the sale of the property on the terms of this contract, undertakes to vacate the property on or before the completion date and releases the property and any included fixtures and contents from any right or interest that the occupier may have note: this condition does not apply to occupiers under leases or tenancies subject to which the property is sold Name(s) and signature(s) of the occupier(s) (if any): Name Signature	Insert the name of Sophia's partner – Andrew Jones	You will recall that Sophia's partner lives at the property with her. Accordingly, his name must be inserted in this special condition. Remember that Sophia's conveyancer will not also advise Andrew due to the risk of a conflict-of-interest

Notices may be sent to: Seller's conveyancer's name: Email address: * Buyers' conveyancer's name Email address: * * Adding an email address authorises service by email see condition 1.3.3 (b)		The name and address of each set of conveyancers is inserted at the bottom of the last page of the contract (often with the reference of the relevant conveyancer) You will note that there is an option to add an email address for each conveyancing firm. Best practice demands that an email address is not added. You will see that adding an email address is confirmation by the conveyancing firm that they will accept service of legal proceedings against their client. Most firms are not willing to take on this responsibility. Accordingly, never include an email address in this part of the contract

Extra special conditions

Both conveyancers should always consider whether any extra special conditions should be drafted and included in the contract. This is because anything that is agreed between the seller and the buyer must be included in the contract for it to be legally binding

Special condition 8	On completion, the buyer will pay the contents price of £2000 (two thousand pounds) for all carpets and curtains at the property	You will recall that Sophia's buyer has agreed to purchase all carpets and curtains for an additional £2000. We included this figure on the front of the contract but, for the avoidance of doubt, it is good practice to include a special condition setting out what has been agreed

Special condition 9	On or before completion, the seller will remove the built-in barbecue in the rear garden of the property and will make good any damage caused	The reason that it is good practice to include this special condition is first that it is something that has been agreed between the parties. Second, if the barbecue is fixed to the ground or cemented in, it could be construed as a 'fixture' which would pass to the buyer on completion in the absence of a contrary condition in the contract.
		The point of considering the terms of the contract carefully, in particular in relation to fixtures and fittings, is to minimise the risk of an argument between the seller and the buyer after completion.

Practice Points

Note that the Protocol provides that the contract should only include 'such additional clauses as are absolutely necessary for the purposes of the transaction' (para 13). This means that CQS accredited firms who are obliged to use the Protocol should not include a large number of additional provisions or amendments to the special conditions as part of their standard contract.

Land law links

A contract is a promise which is legally binding and requires four key elements: offer, acceptance, consideration (that is something of value which a party to the contract is not entitled to already) and intent to create legal relations. Most contracts can be created orally or in writing. The contract for the sale and purchase of land is recognised as being special in that a fifth requirement is required in that it must be in writing. This means that it is not possible to create a contract for the sale and purchase of land orally. The requirement for a contract for the sale of land be in writing is set out in s2 1989 Act.

The reason for this requirement is to ensure that there is a greater degree of certainty relating to the agreement to buy and sell. The contract does not become legally binding until exchange (see Chapter 8).

Next steps

Once the seller's conveyancer has sent the contract package to the buyer's conveyancer, the focus of the transaction and the progression of it then moves to the buyer.

We have seen that if the seller has a mortgage registered over the property, their conveyancer should obtain an indicative redemption figure early in the transaction and certainly prior to exchange of contracts to ensure that the sale price is sufficient to cover costs and mortgages.

Practice Points

Communication with a client is important. It can be helpful to inform a seller that the transaction is likely to go quiet for a few weeks until the buyer's conveyancer has received their search results and raised enquiries (see Chapter 7). Managing a client's expectation is an important part of trying to smooth the process.

Replies to enquiries

We will see that if the buyer's conveyancer has any questions which they want to ask, they will do so by raising 'pre-contract enquiries'. These questions will be sent to the seller's conveyancer who will liaise with their seller client to provide answers to the questions.

Land law links

A seller must understand both when completing the Property Information Form and replying to pre-contract enquiries that the buyer is entitled to rely on the answers that they give. This means that the seller must give honest answers to any questions raised, even if these answers are negative or might deter the buyer from proceeding. If a buyer relies on answers which subsequently turn out to be incorrect, they may be able to sue the seller for misrepresentation after completion.

Practice Points

It is tempting to simply forward any replies to enquiries received by email from the seller to the buyer's conveyancer. This should be avoided. First, the seller's conveyancer should review the answers provided by the seller. Second, simply forwarding an email received from a client to the conveyancer acting for the buyer is a breach of the firm's duty of confidentiality to their seller client because it amounts to sending personal information (the email address) to the other party and their conveyancer.

CHAPTER SEVEN

PROGRESSING A PURCHASE TRANSACTION

Once a conveyancer has taken instructions from their buyer client, they will generally be unable to progress the transaction until the contract pack is received from the seller's conveyancer. The buyer's conveyancer will often give some important advice to the buyer at the beginning of the transaction and this Chapter will consider that advice and the key steps to be taken in relation to the purchase including pre-contract searches and enquiries and financing a purchase.

Stage of the conveyancing process

SELLER	BUYER
PRE-EXCHANGE STAGE OF THE TRANSACTION	
	Obtain money on account for searches
	Submit pre-contract searches, typically: • Local search • Drainage search • Environmental search Are any specialist searches required?

Money on account of searches

A key part of the work of a buyer's conveyancer is carrying out pre-contract searches against the property. These cost money and conveyancing firms will ask their buyer clients to pay money on account of searches. Put simply, this means that the conveyancing firm will ask the buyer to pay for searches upfront.

Practice Points

The LSAG Guidance makes it clear that CDD must be completed before a firm delivers 'substantive work or benefit' for a client or allows property to be transferred. An exception however is that firms can permit funds to be deposited in their client account if they are for fees and disbursements. This means that firms can ask a buyer client for money on account of searches before concluding the identification and AML due diligence procedures. Whether or not a firm chooses to do this is a matter for the firm but receiving any money into client account before conclusion of the due diligence can present a risk.

SDLT questionnaire

SDLT is a tax which must be paid to HMRC if property or land in England and Northern Ireland over a certain price is purchased. If the property is in Wales, Land Transaction Tax is paid if the sale was completed on or after 1 April 2018.

The tax is paid on the purchase of:

- a freehold property
- a new or existing leasehold property
- a property through a shared ownership scheme

It is also payable if property is transferred in exchange for payment for example if a mortgage debt is taken over on a transfer of equity or the share of a house is purchased.

The current threshold for payment of SDLT is £125,000. No SDLT is payable below this figure. A first-time buyer is entitled to SDLT relief. Someone who is buying a property and already owns property will pay a higher rate of SDLT. This has become a complex tax. Conveyancing firms need to obtain information from their buyer clients to enable them to complete the SDLT application on behalf of their clients just after completion (see Chapter 8). To enable them to do this, many firms will send a questionnaire to their buyer client for completion and return.

Practice Points

Dealing with SDLT is a risky area for conveyancing firms, particularly if the client's circumstances change during the transaction. If you become aware of any information on a purchase such as a change in the purchase price or the fact that the buyer owns more than one property, alert a qualified conveyancer as this may change the amount of SDLT payable. The key thing for the conveyancer to understand is whether a buyer owns any other property which they will not be selling. This will impact on the amount of SDLT payable which could increase considerably. Conveyancing firms often advise buyer clients to take detailed accountancy advice prior to exchange of contracts if the SDLT position is not straightforward.

Survey

Buying a house is generally the biggest financial commitment that most people make however, a seller does not have to give a buyer any information as to the structure of any building on the land being purchased. It is for this reason that the conveyancer will advise their buyer client to commission a survey of the property early in the transaction. This will often be done in a standard letter or report. The purpose of a survey is for a surveyor, who is a qualified professional, to attend the property and carry out an inspection of the building. The idea of the survey is to reveal any structural defects or matters which require remedial work. A survey may also confirm the value of the property and whether the boundaries on the ground correspond with those in the title documents.

Importantly, a surveyor owes a duty of care to a client. This means that if a buyer suffers loss as a result of a negligent survey, the buyer can claim against the surveyor for any losses incurred.

Land law links

The seller has to disclose surprisingly little to a buyer when selling a property although the seller must not fraudulently conceal defects or be dishonest when replying to the pre-contract enquiries. The legal principle of 'caveat emptor' applies to property purchases – this means 'let the buyer beware'. It is up to the buyer and their advisers to find out as much as possible about the property prior to exchange of contracts. The discovery of a defect in the title to the property or an adverse search result after exchange of contracts will not give a buyer an automatic right to withdraw from the contract.

Types of survey

There are various types of survey, summarised as follows:

mortgage valuation – this is paid for by the buyer and is an often scant inspection of the property on behalf of the lender to check that the property represents good security for the loan. The buyer should understand that they are not entitled to rely on a mortgage valuation report, even though they have paid for it.

RICS Home Survey Standard (first edition, November 2019) – this is a set of requirements set out by the professional body for surveyors, the RICS, which sets out 3 survey levels:

1. A level 1 survey – this includes a physical inspection of the property and a corresponding report. The report will not include advice on repairs or maintenance. It is offered at a reasonable price and is generally suitable for newer or standard build properties.

2. A level 2 survey – This is also offered at a reasonable price and does not include advice on repairs and maintenance but contains more information than the level 1 survey. This might be suitable for the purchase of older suburban properties, built in the last hundred years also. It does not include a comprehensive comment on the state and condition of the property.

3. A level 3 survey – this is the most expensive of the 3 surveys and provides more information and will include details of maintenance and repairs that are required. This type of survey will be suitable for properties that are older, high value or not of conventional construction.

Practice Points

The Home Survey Reports must be used from 1 September 2021 and replace the RICS Condition Report, HomeBuyer Report and Building

Survey. Conveyancers should review their standard letters and reports to clients to ensure that the up-to-date surveys are referred to.

Further information about the reports can be found on the RICS website' Link:

www.rics.org/uk

Many buyers decide not to commission a survey as this will involve extra cost. The job of the conveyancer is not to insist that the survey is carried out but rather to *advise* that one is carried out. If the client chooses not to do so, it is that their risk.

Conveyancing lawyers are not surveyors and must avoid commenting or advising on a survey result if a buyer provides it. In most survey reports, there is a section covering issues which the legal adviser should check, for example, whether there are any guarantees for new windows or planning permission for building work but this is as far as the conveyancer should go. The buyer must be advised to discuss the content of the survey with the survey if the have any questions.

If the survey reveals significant defects, a buyer may decide to withdraw from the transaction. If the survey reveals work which needs carrying out to the property, the buyer might negotiate with the seller that these works are carried out before completion or might agree a price decrease. If the seller agrees to carry out work between exchange of contracts and completion, this should be included in the contract. If the price paid for the property decreases, any mortgage lender should be informed in writing prior to exchange of contracts.

Often a 'halfway house' is agreed between the buyer and the seller called an 'allowance'. In this situation, the purchase price remains as negotiated but the seller agrees to accept less money from the buyer on completion. The purpose of this is to leave the buyer with some money in hand after completion to carry out the work. An agreed allowance should be reported to any mortgage lender.

Co-ownership

If more than one person is buying a property, the conveyancer must give co-ownership advice. This is often a written report sent early in the transaction. Advice as to the distinction between holding the beneficial interest as joint tenants or tenants in common should be given – see Chapter 1. The conveyancer should advise which form of co-ownership is most appropriate given the client's circumstances. If parties are making unequal contributions towards the purchase price of a property, the conveyancer will often advise that the beneficial interest should be held as tenants in common.

Buyers will often be advised to reflect the detail of their arrangement regarding the beneficial interests in a declaration of trust. They should also be advised to have wills prepared or review existing ones in the light of their purchase.

Practice Points

Buyers often do not want to incur the additional legal fees involved with the preparation of a declaration of trust or will. They should understand that this might represent a risk.

Conveyancers should also be wary of a potential conflict-of-interest between buyers if they cannot agree how the beneficial interest will be held.

Pre-contract searches

You can hopefully start to see that the role of the conveyancer on a purchase is to assist the buyer in gathering information about the property so that the buyer can decide whether or not they want to proceed with the purchase.

A significant part of this information gathering process is the searches which the buyer's conveyancer will carry out fairly early in the transaction and certainly before exchange of contracts. The Protocol suggests that the buyer's conveyancer should submit the searches upon receipt of the draft contract (para 14).

There are various ways to carry out these searches but the most common is to use a commercial organisation that provides searches.

Practice Points

Many conveyancing support staff know how to submit the searches but not why they're doing them. An important part of developing conveyancing skills is to understand the reason for carrying out searches. We will outline below the purpose of most of the key searches.

A very important aspect of risk management is to understand that submitting the searches is not simply a matter of inputting the property address into a commercial search provider's online application form and ticking a few boxes. It is essential for the buyer's conveyancer to consider the location of the property and whether any specialist searches are required in addition to what are considered to be 'standard' searches.

The conveyancer will not be visiting or inspecting the property that their client is purchasing. It is essential for the conveyancer to send the plan of the property to their buyer client prior to submitting the searches to seek the buyer's confirmation that the plan is correct and represents the full extent of the property being purchased.

The searches which most conveyancers will consider 'standard' and will do in every purchase transaction are:

local search – this is a search of records held by the local authority in which the property is situated and will reveal whether there is anything happening on a local level which might adversely affect the property. This comprises 2 forms: the LLC1 (search of local land charges register) and Con29 (enquiries of the local authority). The LLC1 reveals such issues as matters relating to planning, tree preservation orders, smoke control zones. The Con29 reveals issues such as whether the road fronting the property is a publicly adopted highway, public rights-of-way, planning entries, building regulation consents and planning enforcement matters. The Con29 also contains some optional enquiries which will only be answered if requested and an additional fee paid.

Practice Points

An important limitation of the local search is that it only searches against the relevant property address. Despite its name, it does not search against properties in the locality/vicinity and accordingly will not identify issues such as planning permissions relating to adjacent property. This is often a misconception that clients have. They are often keen to know whether there are any current planning permissions relating to property nearby. In this case, the client should be asked whether they want a separate 'plan search', a version of which most commercial search providers will offer.

It is also important to understand the difference between a personal search and an official local search. It is possible to apply for a local search by applying direct to the local authority and paying the appropriate fee. In this case, the local authority will check their records and databases and will supply the result which is known as an 'official search'. If an answer is incorrect on an official search and the buyer suffers loss, they may be able to get recompense from the local authority.

Many local authorities have significant delays in the turnaround of local searches so the commercial search providers offer 'personal searches'. In this event, the search provider carries out the search rather than the local authority accordingly the latter does not guarantee the search result. Most commercial search providers are now members of an industry trade body and maintain insurance against the possibility of a personal search providing incorrect information. This is known as a 'regulated' local search. Most lenders will accept a regulated local search although the conveyancer should check Part 2 of the Lender's Handbook. In any event, the difference between an official search and a personal search should be explained to the buyer.

It is also possible for a conveyancer to carry out a personal search on behalf of their client by attending the local authority themselves although this would be very rare today.

drainage search – this reveal issues such as whether foul water drains into a public sewer, whether the property is connected to the mains water supply and whether any public sewers for within the boundary of the property. Again, it is possible to make a search directly with the water company or through a commercial search provider.

environmental search – this is a search which will provide information such as historic use of the property, flood risk and whether the property is in an area which may be affected by subsidence. There is no standard form and there is a large number of different types of environmental search available from the commercial search providers. An interesting point is that some textbooks do not consider this search to be standard but it is fair to say that the majority of conveyancing firms will carry out an environmental search on every purchase transaction.

Land law links

You can see that a number of the issues covered by the searches also link to land law matters that we have considered. For example, we have seen how important it is to legally be able to gain access to a property. If it abuts (that is, adjoins) the public highway, the buyer is unlikely to have any problems. This is because if a property is adopted by the local authority, there is an automatic right-of-way over it and the local authority will maintain the road. However, if there is an area of land between the boundary of the property and the adopted highway (even if only very narrow), this could cause difficulty if the property does not have a right-of-way over the intervening land.

We have also seen that a residential property needs to benefit from services such as water, foul drainage and electricity. Some of these services are publicly maintained which means that there is an automatic right to use them. However, if the services crossing private land are not maintained by the relevant utility company, further enquiries must be made to deal with this issue.

Practice Points

It is important for the conveyancer to make it clear to the buyer that they are not qualified to interpret the environmental search result. If the result raises issues of concern, the buyer should make further enquiries of the organisations indicated on the search. Other more detailed searches might be required for example, a flood risk report. See below for comments regarding the lenders.

physical inspection of the property – the conveyancer should remind their buyer client of the importance of revisiting the property prior to exchange of contracts to carry out a further physical inspection. It is possible that the only time the buyer has seen the property is when they viewed it with the estate agent prior to putting in an offer. The idea of the physical inspection is for the buyer to remove their 'rose tinted glasses' and to look for issues such as any physical defects in the property (which would then suggest the need for a survey), non-owning occupiers or evidence of third-party rights over the property (for example, a path in the garden).

The most common searches which are not standard and will only be carried out dependent on the transaction or location of the property are:

bankruptcy search against the buyer – this is a search of the bankruptcy register against the full name of all buyers. Generally, this search will be made using the HMLR portal. The cost is £2 per name and the search result comes back immediately. This is carried out if the buyer is getting a mortgage and reveals whether there are any pending or actual bankruptcy proceedings against the buyer. It is a search against the full name so it is possible that a bankruptcy entry could be revealed that is not, in fact, the client of the firm. The conveyancer must make further enquiries in this regard and may need to liaise with the lender. If a bankruptcy entry is revealed which relates to the buyer, this will mean that the transaction is not proceeding. Note that this search must be repeated before completion (see Chapter 8).

common's registration search – this is one of the optional Con29 searches and reveals whether the land has been registered as a common or a town or village green. This is significant because third parties may have rights over common land, for example rights to graze cattle and there are issues relating to vehicular access over common land. This search should be carried out if the property is next to open land or a village green or is a new build.

coal mining search – as the name implies, this will be carried out if the property is in an area which is affected by coalmining or historic mining. The purpose is to establish whether there are any mines beneath the property which might affect the structural stability of the property.

chancel search – a court case held that landowners could be responsible for contributing towards the upkeep of the chancel (the space around the altar) in the local church. This is an ancient obligation which few solicitors thought about until a legal case in 2003 which established that it is still possible for a demand to be made of the property owners in the locality for a contribution to the upkeep of the chancel. The problem is that this liability often does not appear on the title deeds and could run to hundreds if not thousands of pounds for affected properties. The official records of affected properties are incomplete so indemnity insurance has become the solution to this issue. A chancel search will reveal whether the establish property is in an area considered to be at risk of chancel liability. If a positive result is forthcoming, the conveyancer should raise the issue of indemnity insurance. Some firms have a 'blanket' insurance policy in place which covers all properties upon which they are instructed. The situation is somewhat more complex since 2013 and some firms do not carry out chancel searches any more.

company search – if the seller is a limited company (for example a developer on a new build transaction) it is necessary to carry out a company search to check that the company exists and is able to deal with land transactions.

There is a miscellany of other searches which could be carried out dependent on the location of the property. The commercial search provider might flag these. The conveyancer should also consider the geographical location of the property to establish whether any other non-standard searches might be appropriate.

Stage of the conveyancing process

SELLER	BUYER
PRE-EXCHANGE STAGE OF THE TRANSACTION	
	Submit pre-contract searches, typically: • Local search • Drainage search • Environmental search Are any specialist searches required?
	Investigate title Receive and review search results
	Raise pre-contract enquiries
Liaise with seller and reply to pre-contract enquiries	

Title investigation

The buyer's conveyancer will investigate the seller's title in parallel with carrying out the pre-contract searches. We have seen in Chapter 4 the main issues which might arise on the purchase of a residential freehold property with a registered title. Review the content of the register if necessary.

The conveyancer must also review the draft contract to ensure that it:

- contains the agreed purchase price
- accords with the buyer's instructions
- correctly identifies the seller
- refers correctly and comprehensively to the title
- contains all agreed terms (such as confirmation that a non-owning occupier will move out or that the seller will carry out specified works between exchange and completion or will provide an indemnity insurance policy)
- has the Fittings and Contents form affixed to it

Review the contract in Chapter 6.

Review of other documents

The conveyancer should send the Protocol forms and any other documents such as guarantees to the buyer client for review. The conveyancer should also check these documents and note any discrepancies or points of concern.

Raising pre-contract enquiries

If the conveyancer or their buyer client have any concerns or questions about any of the documents referred to above, the buyer's conveyancer must send these questions to the seller's conveyancer. These are called 'pre-contract enquiries'.

There is no 'magic' to raising enquiries but it is important to ensure that any enquiry is well drafted and specific, to elicit a meaningful response. Let's look at a few examples of some common enquiries which the buyer's conveyancer may need to raise and contrast a poorly drafted enquiry with something more focused:

Issue	Poor enquiry	Notes / alternative enquiry
A conveyance containing covenants is on the charges register of title but no copy has been supplied with the contract pack	We note that entry 3 of the charges register refers to a conveyance containing covenants.	This is not an enquiry it is an observation. It does not ask the seller's conveyancer to do anything. A facetious but correct response might be: 'We note that you note this'. The above is, of course, a completely unhelpful reply. A better enquiry would be: We note that entry 3 of the charges register of title number SK98765 refers to a conveyance containing covenants but a copy of the conveyance was not contained in the contract pack. Please provide a copy of the conveyance.

The seller has agreed to provide indemnity insurance regarding undisclosed covenants	We understand from our client that the seller has agreed to provide indemnity insurance on completion.	Again, this is completely non-specific and is merely a statement that does not require any action. A better enquiry would be: We understand that the seller has agreed to provide indemnity insurance regarding the undisclosed covenants referred to at entry 2 of the charges register of title number SK98765. Please confirm that this is agreed and if so, supply a draft indemnity policy for our consideration and please draft a special condition for insertion into the contract.
The local search reveals that the road fronting the property is not an adopted highway	Our local search has revealed that the road fronting the property is not an adopted highway	This is another poor enquiry but, importantly, it also raises an issue of significant risk which an inexperienced conveyancer should pass to a colleague. In this situation, it would be necessary to check the property register of the title to establish whether the property enjoys a right-of-way over the road fronting the property. It is also likely to involve indemnity insurance and a statutory declaration or statement of truth. We have deliberately not included an alternative, better, enquiry for this situation because each transaction will turn on its own facts.

Practice Points

Note that CQS accredited firms should not raise indiscriminate pre-contract enquiries. They should only raise enquiries which are specific to the documentation supplied. The Protocol states as follows:

'Raise only specific additional enquiries required to clarify issues arising out of the documents submitted, or which are relevant to the title, existing or planned use, nature or location of the property or which the buyer has expressly requested.

Do not raise any additional enquiries about the state and condition of the building unless arising out of your conveyancing search results, your buyer's own enquiries, inspection or their surveyor's report.

Indiscriminate use of 'standard' additional enquiries may constitute a breach of this Protocol. If such enquiries are submitted, they are not required to be dealt with by the seller/seller's conveyancer.

The seller's conveyancer does not need to obtain the seller's answers to any enquiry seeking opinion rather than fact.' (para 15)

A significant risk in relation to a purchase is to ensure that all pre-contract enquiries have been raised but, importantly, that they have also been properly answered. A key part of the skill of the conveyancer is to recognise when an answer or solution is acceptable. If you are in any doubt as to this, you should refer the matter to a qualified conveyancer or more experienced colleague. Under no circumstances should the transaction proceed to exchange of contracts until all such results have been received and pre-contract enquiries have been comprehensively answered.

Stage of the conveyancing process

SELLER	BUYER
PRE-EXCHANGE STAGE OF THE TRANSACTION	
	Resolve how the buyer will finance the purchase: • Cash and/or • Mortgage

Financing a purchase

Most buyers of a residential property in England and Wales will fund the purchase with a combination of cash from their own resources and a mortgage from an institutional lender such as a High Street bank or building society. We have seen that client money on a transaction must be paid into a conveyancing firm's client account and we have considered the steps that must be taken to check the source of funds and source of wealth in relation to any cash which the client is putting towards the purchase.

Many buyers will have a 'related' sale transaction and their conveyancer will act on the sale and the purchase. Transactions being 'related' means that a property owner needs to sell the property that they are living in to fund the purchase of their next home. Typically, these transactions will need to happen on the same day – so that the property owner can move from one house to another on the same date – this is known as 'synchronising' the transactions. A conveyancer must ensure that they synchronise the transactions otherwise a person could end up homeless or, possibly worse, owning one property and defaulting on the purchase of another. In many cases, when a property owner sells their property, once the costs, fees and any mortgage is paid off, there is some money left over to put towards the related purchase; this money is called the 'net sale proceeds'. We have seen above that from an AML point of view, the sale proceeds forming part of the funds for a purchase represents a lower risk than, say, cash, because the source of the money can be easily identified.

The Mortgage Offer

Once a buyer has an offer to purchase a property accepted, they will often use the services of a mortgage broker to assist them with finding a suitable mortgage product. The broker will take details of the buyer's financial position and needs and will check the mortgage market to find a product which meets those needs. The broker will often assist the buyer to gather together their financial information to submit an application to a mortgage lender for a mortgage. The lender will carry out credit reference checks and will assess the buyer's ability to meet the mortgage payments; if the lender concludes that the buyer meets their criteria, they will set down the terms upon which they are prepared to lend money to the buyer in a document called a 'mortgage offer'.

Mortgage offers from most mainstream lenders follow a similar format and include the following information:

- full name of the buyer (borrower)
- address of the property being purchased over which the mortgage will be secured
- purchase price of property
- amount of the mortgage loan
- term of the loan – most residential mortgages are 25 years in duration
- interest rate which will be applied to the capital sum borrowed
- type of mortgage product – for example, whether capital and repayment or interest only (see below)
- monthly payments to be paid by the buyer (borrower)
- whether there are any early repayment charges (often referred to as 'early redemption penalties'). A borrower can pay off their mortgage loan before the end of the term, but in some cases will be required to pay a penalty for this early repayment
- any special conditions which apply to the particular mortgage offer (see below)

Types of mortgage product

There are many different types of mortgage product available to buyers, some of the most common are:

repayment – this is the most common type of mortgage and is a product where the monthly payments cover part capital repayment and part interest so the loan is paid off at the end of the mortgage term

interest only – this is often the cheapest mortgage product and is one where the borrower only makes interest payments each month. The borrower must understand that the capital sum borrowed will remain outstanding for the full term of the loan and they will need to be able to pay this sum of at the end of the term

pension mortgage – this is a product that is linked to the borrower's pension and is sometimes used if the borrower is self-employed

Practice Points

The conveyancer may liaise with the mortgage broker at the beginning of the transaction but once the lender has issued a mortgage offer, generally the broker is no longer involved because their job is done.

There is a very important limitation on the advice which conveyancing firms can give to buyers in relation to their mortgage offer. We will see (below) that the conveyancer must carry out checks on behalf of the lender and give certain advice to the buyer but a conveyancer must not give specific financial advice about a particular lender or mortgage product. This is because most conveyancing firms do not have the appropriate authorisation to give financial advice. We can give generic advice as part of our legal advice but a conveyancer must not go on to recommend, for example, that their buyer client might be better obtaining a different mortgage product from a different lender.

In straightforward terms, a solicitor or licensed conveyancer can tell a client what entering into the mortgage agreement means and the consequences of default but they cannot tell the client whether or not it is a good deal or recommend an alternative.

The position of the lender

The lender will usually issue two copies of the mortgage offer: one to the buyer and one to their conveyancing firm. This is because the buyer's conveyancer will usually act for the lender as well as the buyer. The firm will need to be on the 'panel' of conveyancers that the lender is willing to use. If not, the buyer's lender may insist on using another firm – this is known as 'separate representation' (this is rare in a residential conveyancing transaction).

The lender becomes a client of the firm. However, the lender will not be treated like a typical client because they will not receive a client care letter (see Chapter 2) nor will the lender pay the firm any legal fees. The firm owes duties to the lender and the buyer. It is generally permissible for the buyer's conveyancer to act for the lender because there is no conflict of interest between them. Both parties want the same thing – a good and marketable title for the property being purchased. A buyer needs a good title to enable them to sell the property in the future. A lender needs a good title to enable them to sell the property in the event that they repossess the property due to default by the buyer.

UK Finance Mortgage Lenders Handbook ('Lender's Handbook')

This sets out comprehensive instructions for conveyancers acting on behalf of lenders in residential conveyancing transactions. It used to be called the Council of Mortgage Lenders (CML) Handbook. The Lender's Handbook sets out the steps that the conveyancer acting for the lender has to comply with when dealing with the purchase and the mortgage. Part 1 of the Handbook contains instructions for every transaction. If a lender wants to modify these standard instructions, they will do this in Part 2 of the Handbook, which sets out each individual lender's changes to Part 1. The Handbook also has Part 3 instructions which deals with the situation where the buyer and lender are separately represented, but this is rare in a residential conveyancing transaction.

The Lender's Handbook is voluntary for lenders and not all of them choose to use it, in this case, the lender will set out its own instructions for the conveyancer. However, most lenders which conveyancers will commonly encounter adopt the Lender's Handbook.

The Building Societies Association has produced an alternative set of mortgage instructions (sometimes referred to as the BSA Handbook). Again, these are a standard set of instructions which conveyancers acting for the lenders adopting the BSA Handbook must follow. Currently, 28 organisations, mostly building societies, use these instructions.

In both cases, the instructions contain similar obligations with which the conveyancer acting for the lender must comply. There are a large number of issues for the conveyancer to deal with and some of the most important in the Lender's Handbook are:

- conveyancers should use the particular lender's standard documents (for example, the mortgage deed) and must not amend them without consent – 1.11

- all communications between the conveyancer and the lender should be in writing, quoting the mortgage account number, the surname and initials of the borrower and property address. Copies of all written communications should be retained on file – 2.1

- conveyancers must follow the rules of their professional body and comply with AML requirements – 3.1.2
- unless a conveyancer personally knows the borrower or signatory, the borrower must provide evidence of identity – 3.1.5
- the conveyancer should advise the borrower that the borrower should not rely on the mortgage valuation report – 4.4
- the conveyancer must report to the lender immediately if the registered proprietor of the property has owned the property for less than six months (there are exceptions such as a sale by personal representatives) – 5.1
- conflicts of interest must be avoided – 5.3
- the conveyancer must carry out all usual and necessary searches and enquiries and must report any adverse entries to the lender – 5.4.1
- the title to the property must be good and marketable – 5.6.1
- on completion the lender requires a fully enforceable first legal charge over the property – 5.12.1
- the conveyancer must ask the borrower how the balance of the purchase price is being provided; if the funds are not coming from the borrower's own resources (for example, due to a gift from parents) this must be reported to the lender – 5.13.1
- the purchase price for the property is appearing in the contract and transfer must be the same as set out in the lenders mortgage instructions – 6.3.1
- the property must be vacant on completion (unless it is a buy to let mortgage product) – 6.5.1
- the conveyancer must not submit the Certificate of Title unless it is unqualified or, if an issue has been raised with the lender, they have authorised the conveyancer in writing to proceed – 10.1
- the conveyancer is only authorised to release the mortgage funds to the seller's conveyancer on completion when they hold

sufficient funds to complete purchase of the property and pay all SDLT as well as having the HMLR fees to enable the conveyancer to register the legal charge – 10.4

- before the mortgage advance is released on completion, the conveyancer must hold a completed SDLT form signed by the borrower or the borrower's authority to allow the conveyancer to make the necessary application on completion and the borrower's behalf – 10.5

- the conveyancer must ensure that the SDLT and HMLR applications are made within the appropriate timeframes – 10.6

- the conveyancer must ensure that the mortgage deed is properly signed and witnessed by an independent person – 11.2.1

- after completion, the conveyancer must register the lender's mortgage as a first legal charge over the property with HMLR – 14.1.1

Reporting to the lender

If a conveyancer acting for a lender discovers an issue about the property which is adverse, the conveyancer is under a duty to report such matters to the lender. Examples might be a breach of planning permission, a title defect or no legal access to the property. The conveyancer should inform their buyer client of the need to report a matter to the lender prior to making any report. Once an issue has been reported to the lender, the conveyancer should not exchange contracts (see Chapter 8), until they have received written confirmation from the lender that they can proceed.

A key risk for conveyancers is that they receive an unhelpful or fairly meaningless response from the lender, such as: 'We will rely on you to protect our security'. Conveyancers should always be on the lookout for this sort of response from the lender. An answer in these terms is simply passing the risk back to the conveyancing firm. It may be that the conveyancer has to contact the lender again to ask them to confirm that the matter can proceed in spite of the issue that has been reported. Best practice demands that conveyancers obtain authority to proceed from the lender in writing and that they do not rely on a telephone conversation in this regard.

Practice Points

When reporting matters to a lender, the conveyancer must be aware of the possibility of a conflict-of-interest arising between the lender and the buyer. If the buyer refuses to allow the conveyancer to make this report, the conveyancer must refuse to continue to act for the lender. This will generally involve the conveyancer returning the mortgage offer to the lender without further comment. A conveyancer owes a duty of confidentiality to their buyer so they should ensure that they have the buyer's consent to notify the lender of any relevant issues prior to making contact with the lender.

Mortgage report

Most conveyancing firms will send their client a mortgage report, outlining such things as:

- The general terms of the mortgage offer
- Whether the mortgage product is interest only or repayment, for example
- The rate/s of interest that apply
- Whether there are any early redemption penalties
- A request to sign the mortgage deed
- The requirement for the buyer to keep the property insured and in good repair
- The requirement that the buyer does not alter or extend the property without the lender's consent
- The requirements for the buyer to keep up the mortgage repayments – otherwise the lender will be able to repossess the property

Practice Points

Remember that conveyancers can only give generic mortgage advice. We cannot give specific mortgage advice. This means that we can advise as to the type of mortgage above and can tell the client in general terms about their mortgage offer. However, we cannot comment on whether the mortgage offer represents a good deal for the client and we cannot recommend particular products from particular lenders. We must advise the buyer to take independent financial advice in this case.

The Lender's Handbook and searches

The Lender's Handbook does not specify what searches the conveyancer should carry out. The lenders leave this to the discretion of the conveyancer which, of course, leaves the liability with the conveyancer. Section 5.4 of the Lender's Handbook deals with searches and reports and states that:

- the conveyancer must ensure that all 'usual and necessary searches and enquiries' have been carried out (5.4.1)
- the conveyancer must report any adverse entry to the lender but the lender does not want the search itself (5.4.1)
- the lender must be named as applicant in the HMLR search (5.4.1) – see Chapter 8
- the conveyancer must carry out any other searches which may be appropriate to the property taking into account locality and other features (5.4.2)
- all searches must not be more than 6 months old completion except where there is a priority period (5.4.3)
- the conveyancer must inform the lender of any contaminated land entries and should check Part 2 of the Handbook to see if the particular lender wants to receive the search result or report (5.4.4)
- the conveyancer must check Part 2 of the Handbook to see if the lender accepts personal searches (5.4.5) or search insurance (5.4.6)

Mortgage documents

The mortgage offer will contain a standard mortgage deed which all of the borrowers are required to sign. Note that this is a deed so the borrower's signature is must be witnessed by an independent person. Most conveyancing firms will ensure that their buyer clients have signed the mortgage deed prior to exchange of contracts or, at the very latest, prior to completion.

The mortgage offer will also contain a standard document called a 'Certificate of Title'. The purpose of this document is twofold. First it acts as confirmation that the conveyancing firm has complied with all of the requirements in the Lender's Handbook and that the title to the property is good and marketable. Second, it acts as a request for the mortgage advance. Most lenders require the conveyancer to submit the Certificate of Title at least 5 or 7 working days prior to the completion date. This is significant because if the conveyancer gives less notice than the lender requires, the conveyancer might not receive the mortgage advance in time for completion. This will put their buyer client in breach of contract.

Practice Points

Most lenders now use a portal called Lender Exchange through which most communication regarding mortgage products takes place between the conveyancing firm and the lender. The conveyancing firm must ensure that they submit the Certificate of Title to the lender in the format and via the medium required by the lender. Some will still accept a Certificate of Title sent by fax. If a conveyancer is in any doubt, they should check the lender's particular requirements prior to exchange of contracts.

Completing the mortgage

As we will see in Chapter 8, on the day of completion, the buyer's conveyancer should be holding the total sum required to enable them to complete their client's purchase, which is usually 90% of the purchase price plus all fees and outgoings. Remember that 10% of the purchase price is paid on exchange of contracts. Remember also that the Lender's Handbook requires the conveyancing firm to have the SDLT and HMLR fees in its client account prior to using the mortgage advance on the day of completion. The buyer's conveyancer will send the sum required to complete transaction by telegraphic transfer to the seller's conveyancer. Once completion has taken place, the buyer's conveyancer will insert the date of completion into the mortgage deed which they should already be holding on their file. This will be sent to HMLR with the application for registration – see Chapter 8.

Land Law Links

We have seen that a mortgage is an interest in land given by the mortgagor (land owner) as security for a loan. The mortgagor receives a loan in return for giving the mortgagee (usually an institutional lender such as a bank or building society) security over the land. This security takes the form of a legal charge which affects the title. A legal mortgage must be created by deed and in most cases, the terms of the mortgage will give the lender a 'power of sale'. If the borrower defaults on the mortgage repayments, the lender will have the right to take the property back from the landowner. They will obtain a court order which will give them the right to sell the property to recover the loan which remains unpaid.

A legal mortgage must be protected. If the title to the property is unregistered (see Chapter 4), the lender will retain the original title deeds as security for the loan. If the title to the property is registered (see Chapter 4) the mortgage must be registered against the charges register of the affected title.

Practice Points

Note that residential conveyancing work is generally non-contentious. This means that residential conveyancers do not do work which involves litigation or court proceedings. We are generally involved with a mortgage when it is created and one of the obligations when acting for a lender under the terms of the Lender's Handbook is to ensure that the lender's security is protected by registration. If a borrower defaults on a mortgage, this will generally be handled by a litigation department and not a residential conveyancing department.

CHAPTER EIGHT
EXCHANGE TO POST COMPLETION

You can see from the Chapter title that we are going to cover a significant amount of the transaction in a short time. In the context of an average conveyancing transaction this is realistic. As we have seen, the due diligence and identification processes at the beginning of the transaction can be time-consuming and certainly risky. Once we have taken instructions, the bulk of the work carried out by the conveyancers is between confirmation of instructions and exchange of contracts – this is likely to take a few weeks. Once the buyer's conveyancer has received all of the search results, replies to enquiries and has resolved the financing, the parties will approach exchange of contracts. This is the stage in the transaction where the matter becomes legally binding. The completion date is also fixed and there is often as little as one or two weeks between exchange of contracts and completion. After the clients have moved in to their new property, the conveyancers have some important work to do. This Chapter will consider these parts of the conveyancing process.

Stage of the conveyancing process

SELLER	BUYER
PRE-EXCHANGE STAGE OF THE TRANSACTION	
	Report to client on the title, search results and replies to enquiries
	Obtain funds from the buyer for the deposit paid on exchange of contracts, typically 10% of the purchase price
Seller and buyer agree suitable moving date (completion date) and inform their conveyancer	

Preparing for exchange of contracts

We have seen that the seller's conveyancer will wait for pre-contract enquiries, if any, once the contract pack has been submitted. There is much more for the buyer's conveyancer to do. We saw in Chapter 7 the work which the buyer's conveyancer must carry out.

Report to buyer

The buyer's conveyancer must also report to their client on their findings. They might do this as they go along or will wait until all search results and replies to pre-contract enquiries have been received. The buyer's conveyancer should report to their client on the following:

Title to the property

Send a copy of the title

Advise on tenure, rights and obligations

Boundaries

Send a copy of the title plan

Advise as to boundary maintenance if known – this might be referred to in the title and the seller should have indicated which boundaries they have maintained in question 1 of the Property Information Form

Search results

Send copies of the search results

Advise as to results for example: is the road fronting the property adopted? Enclose planning permissions, is the property connected to public foul drainage and water supply? Are there any adverse matters on the environmental search?

Information about the property

Send copies of the Property Information Form, Fittings and Contents Form, planning permissions and guarantees, EPC, enquiries and replies.

As we have seen, the conveyancer should ensure that the client has considered having a survey carried out and if they have, whether they are satisfied with the condition of the property. The conveyancer will report on the mortgage offer if any and will ensure that they are clear as to co-ownership requirements if more than one buyer.

Practice Points

Most conveyancing firms will have standard reports to send to the clients to deal with the above matters. It is important to ensure, however that the specifics relating to the property are brought to the client's attention and the client must understand what they have been told.

An important and often blurred distinction between the conveyancer and their client is that the conveyancer advises, the client instructs. A buyer will often say to their conveyancer: 'What if your opinion? Would *you* buy this house?'. The conveyancer should not offer an opinion. The conveyancer should advise on what they have found out and explain the risks in language their client can understand and invite the client to instruct them as to whether or not the client wants to proceed.

Contract and deposit

At the beginning of the transaction, the contract is drafted by the seller's conveyancer and is sent in duplicate to the buyer's conveyancer. During the transaction the terms of the contract are agreed including the insertion of the buyer's full name and any specific issues agreed between seller and buyer. Each conveyancer will end up with an identical part of the contract which they will have signed by their respective clients in readiness for exchange. Any non-owning occupier living at the property to be sold should also sign the seller's part of the contract (their details will be inserted in special condition 7 of contract).

On exchange of contracts, the buyer will typically pay 10% of the purchase price as a deposit. This is effectively a down payment. The buyer's conveyancer must arrange for their client to pay the deposit to the firm. This will often be as a bank transfer of cash direct into the firm's client account. The deposit must be cleared funds before the buyer's conveyancer can rely on it otherwise this will be a breach of the Accounts Rules.

Property insurance

In most residential conveyancing transactions, the risk passes to the buyer upon exchange. This means that the buyer should arrange for buildings insurance to be put on place immediately exchange of contracts has taken place. Often, a property is insured by both the seller and the buyer between exchange of contracts and completion. The seller should leave their own buildings insurance in place between exchange and completion, particularly if they have a mortgage over the property.

The buyer's conveyancer may ask their buyer client for evidence that the buildings insurance has been put on risk and must do so if a lender imposes this obligation on the conveyancer and the Lender's Handbook.

Completion statements

Both conveyancers should prepare a completion statement for their respective clients showing the financial position regarding the transactions. Best practice demands that draft figures are prepared by the conveyancers before exchange of contracts which are then finalised after exchange of contracts (see below).

Stage of the conveyancing process

SELLER	BUYER
EXCHANGE STAGE OF THE TRANSACTION	
This is the point at which the transaction becomes legally binding. The buyer pays 10% of the purchase price as the deposit on exchange and the completion date (the moving date) is agreed and inserted into the contract.	
EXCHANGE	EXCHANGE

Exchange of contracts

This is a key stage in the transaction when the matter becomes legally binding between the seller and the buyer. You can see how much work the conveyancers have carried out from taking instructions to this point in the transaction. It is important to realise that at any point prior to exchange of contracts, the seller or buyer could withdraw from the transaction without any financial penalty to the other. Once exchange of contracts takes place, it is legally binding and financial penalties will be incurred if the seller or buyer withdraw from the transaction after exchange of contracts.

Authority to exchange

It is essential for a conveyancer to obtain their client's irrevocable authority to proceed to exchange of contracts, ideally in writing. It is also best practice to obtain the client's authority to exchange on the day of exchange of contracts itself. If exchange does not happen on a particular day, the conveyancer should refresh their client's authority to exchange the next day. Clients have been known to change their mind (or, worse, die) overnight. A conveyancer who exchanges contracts without their client's authority could be negligent.

Practice Points

As exchange of contracts is the 'point of no return', you should also obtain the authority of all of your clients on a particular file to exchange and should keep a written note of the fact that you obtained the authority on your file.

Methods of exchange

It is possible to exchange contracts in person with the conveyancer on the other side of the transaction but for logistical reasons this is fairly rare these days. It is also technically possible to exchange using the post but the uncertainty of this method means that it is never used. Unsurprisingly, the method of exchange which is most frequently used is exchange on the telephone. This involves the conveyancers acting for seller and buyer having a conversation with each other and during the conversation, exchange of contracts takes place.

Land law links

Interestingly, the courts have only recognised telephone as a valid method of exchanging contracts since the case of *Domb v Isoz [1980]*. Whilst this is no doubt well before most people reading this Practical Guide were born, telephones were in widespread use well before this date!

Who should exchange contracts?

We have seen that both sale and purchase file should be carefully reviewed to ensure that there are no outstanding matters before exchange of contracts. The seller and buyer must also agree the completion date (that is, the moving date) between themselves. Obviously if there is a chain of transactions and a number of sellers and buyers involved, they must all agree the same moving date.

There is often a significant pressure from everyone involved in the chain at the point just before exchange of contracts. It is a very stressful time and conveyancers are often on the receiving end of this stress. Exchange of contracts is the point of legal commitment therefore only a suitably qualified conveyancer or someone with sufficient experience should exchange contracts on behalf of their clients.

Practice Points

An inexperienced conveyancer should never be pressurised by a lawyer on the other side of the transaction or an estate agent or indeed, client, to exchange contracts if they do not have the authority or the experience to do so.

If a client has a related sale and purchase, they will usually want to synchronise the exchange and completion. This means that the conveyancer must ensure that exchange and completion happen on both files on the same day to enable the client to move from one house to the other on the agreed completion date. In some cases, a seller might be willing to proceed on their sale independently of their purchase. We have seen throughout this Practical Guide that the conveyancer must make no assumptions as to their client's intentions. If the client is willing to effectively 'break the chain' and go ahead on their sale without tying in their purchase, their conveyancer must obtain written instructions from their client confirming that they are willing to do this.

The client must understand that if they proceed to exchange on their sale, there is no guarantee that the purchase will ever catch up or happen. The seller will be contractually obliged to move out of the house that they are selling on the completion date and will need arrangements for storage of the furniture and somewhere to stay.

Formulae for exchange

When all of the above steps are concluded the conveyancer is finally ready to exchange contracts. You can see that a client becoming committed to a significant financial transaction on the basis of a telephone call is risky. The parties to the telephone call could become distracted, forget what was said or simply not agree with each other as to the content of the telephone conversation. These uncertainties led to the development by the Law Society of the formulae for exchange. Essentially, these are a set of steps which the conveyancers carrying out the exchange of contracts on the telephone must follow to provide both certainty and evidence as to what happened. There are 3 formulae:

Formula A is used where one conveyancer holds both parts of the contract; one signed by the seller and one signed by buyer). This is relatively unusual today.

Formula B is used where each conveyancer holds their clients signed part of the contract

Formula C is used where there is a chain of transactions and involves 2 telephone calls; one call to set up the exchange and the second to confirm the exchange. This is a more complex, risky process and involves the deposit being passed down the chain.

During the telephone call, the conveyancers must go through the contract and confirm that they are holding an identical contract. The buyer's conveyancer will confirm the amount of the deposit to be paid. At the point they are ready to exchange, they will insert the date of the telephone call in the section of the contract marked 'date' and will insert the agreed completion date into the contract in the section of the contract marked 'completion'. These dates will be handwritten by the conveyancers.

Only when all this has been done will the conveyancers agree that exchange of contracts has taken place and they will note the formulae used and the time for exchange in the contract. There is a box on the top right-hand corner of the front page of the contract in which the conveyancers will write the names of the conveyancers who had the telephone call to exchange, the formula used and the time of exchange of contracts.

All of the formulae also require the conveyancers to make a written memorandum of exchange of contracts to be placed on the file. The memorandum should include the following:

- the date and time of exchange
- the formula used and exact wording of agreed variations
- the completion date
- the deposit to be paid
- the identities of the conveyancers involved in the conversation

Use of all of the formulae involves implied undertakings which is another reason exchange is risky and must be carried out by someone with suitable experience. Each conveyancer undertakes that they will send their clients signed part of the contract to the other on the day of exchange and in addition, the buyer's conveyancer is also undertaking that they will send the agreed deposit to the seller's conveyancer on the day of exchange.

If it is not possible to comply with any of the implied undertakings, the conveyancers must vary the undertakings just before exchange takes place.

Practice Points

It has become common practice for exchange to take place without the agreed deposit actually being paid over by the buyer's conveyancer to the seller's conveyancer. The conveyancers often just agree that the deposit is 'held to order' often without understanding the implications of this wording. The effect of this statement is that the conveyancer is giving an undertaking that they will pay the deposit to the conveyancer on the other side on demand. This is risky for the buyer's conveyancer because they might not actually hold any money in their client account but is simply relying on a similar undertaking given on their related sale. This is a further reminder of the risk of exchange of contracts.

Immediately after exchange of contracts

Both conveyancers must inform their clients that exchange of contracts has taken place and the buyer will be advised to put their buildings insurance on risk. Both conveyancers must also comply with the undertakings given on exchange and send the contract and deposit (if acting for the buyer) on the day of exchange.

Practice Points

Ensure that the agreed date of completion is properly diarised whether on a case management system, paper diary or the file. It is important from a risk management point of view for conveyancing firms to maintain a central record of key dates such as completion to ensure that they are not missed. It is not sufficient for the individual fee earner dealing with the file to know about the completion date. How would colleagues know about a completion date if that fee earner is unexpectedly away from the office on any given completion date?

Stage of the conveyancing process

SELLER	BUYER
PRE-COMPLETION (OR POST EXCHANGE) STAGE OF THE TRANSACTION Often there are two weeks between exchange of contracts and completion	
Obtain redemption figure on seller's mortgage (if any)	
	Draft transfer
Approve transfer Seller to sign transfer	
Prepare completion statement	Prepare completion statement Obtain funds to complete: • Request any cash due from buyer and/or • Submit Certificate of Title to lender
	Submit pre- completion searches: • Bankruptcy search (if buyer is getting a mortgage) • HMLR Official search with priority (OS1) **RISK!** It is essential to ensure that the 30-working day OS1 priority period expiry is diarised
Fill in Completion Information and Undertakings Form (2019) **RISK!** Who is authorised to give the undertaking to redeem the seller's mortgage/s?	Check Completion Information and Undertakings Form (2019) to ensure that the seller's conveyancer has given an undertaking to pay off all of the seller's mortgages from the sale proceeds

Preparing for completion

<u>Seller's conveyancer – redemption figure</u>

If the seller has a mortgage over their property, we saw that at the beginning of the transaction that an important part of risk management is for the seller's conveyancer to obtain an indicative redemption figure prior to exchange of contracts. You will remember that the point of this is for the seller's conveyancer to ensure that they have sufficient funds to pay off the mortgage on completion.

Once exchange of contracts has taken place, the completion date is fixed. Accordingly, the seller's conveyancer must contact the lender to request a redemption figure calculated to the completion date.

Once this figure has been obtained, the seller's conveyancer can prepare an up-to-date completion statement showing the exact net sale proceeds. This should be sent to the seller for approval.

<u>Buyer's conveyancer – the draft transfer</u>

The buyer's conveyancer will draft the transfer. This is the document which will transfer the legal title from the seller to the buyer on completion. Some conveyancers will prepare the transfer prior to exchange of contracts but traditionally it has been drafted following exchange of contracts and before completion.

A sample TR1 is below using the parties to the contract which was drafted in Chapter 6.

The draft transfer will be sent to the seller's conveyancer for approval. If they have any amendments to make, they will send the amendments back to the buyer's conveyancer. In many cases, this is done by email these days.

Practice Points

It is essential for the seller's conveyancer to ensure that their seller client has signed the transfer in readiness for completion.

Let's look at the standard clauses required in the TR1 and then consider the completed draft.

1. Title number – insert the title number of the property

2. Property – insert the postal address of the property. This must accord with the address as it appears on the property register of the title

3. Date – on drafting, the date of the transfer is left blank. This is the completion date which will be inserted in writing by the seller's conveyancer on the day of completion

4. Transferor – insert the full name of the seller as it appears in the contract

5. Transferee – insert the full name of the buyer as it appears in the contract

Land law links

Remember that the legal title can only be held by a maximum of 4 people who are of sound mind and over the age of 18. Accordingly, only 4 people can appear as transferees in the transfer

6. Transferee's intended address for service – This is the address which will appear on the proprietorship register. You will remember that at 3 addresses can be included (which includes an email address). Typically, the address of the property will be inserted. However, if the buyer is not going to live at the property on completion (for example, because it is an investment/buy to let property) then the buyer's home address should be inserted in addition to the property address. This is very important because this is the address which HMLR will use to contact the property owner in the event that a notice has to be sent to them

7. You do not need to insert anything into this box but it contains essential wording. This is known as the 'operative' part of the deed as it is the wording which transfers the legal title from the seller to the buyer

8. Consideration – this is the purchase price for the property as it appears in the contract. You will see that it needs to be inserted in words and figures

9. Title guarantee – check the box for either full or limited title guarantee – this must be as per the contract. Remember that a seller who has lived in the property will generally give a full title guarantee. A personal representative selling a property in a probate sale will give a limited title guarantee

10. Declaration of trust – if there are two or more buyers, they will receive co-ownership advice and this box must be completed in accordance with the client's instructions

11. Additional provisions – if it is necessary to include extra clauses in the TR1, they will be inserted in box 11. You will recall from the register of title in Chapter 4, that Sophia Carol Hayward gave an indemnity covenant when she purchased the property (see entry 5 of the proprietorship register), accordingly she is entitled to demand an indemnity covenant from her buyer. If it is necessary to appoint a second trustee to effect overreaching, the appointment of the second trustee will be included in box 11

12. Execution – this is the part of the transfer where the signatures appear. All sellers must always sign every transfer. It is essential that the seller's conveyancer holds a transfer signed by all sellers on the day of completion and certainly before any funds are released to the seller. If there is just one transferee, they will need to sign if there is an indemnity covenant in box 11. If there is more than one transferee, they will all need to sign the transfer as evidence of their agreement to the co-ownership declaration in box 10 and, additionally, as confirmation that they agree to the indemnity covenant if included.

See also HMLR's guidance on completing the TR1. Link:

https://www.gov.uk/government/publications/registered-titles-whole-transfer-tr1/guidance-completing-form-tr1-for-the-transfer-of-registered-property

Let's assume that the buyers are Michael and Jean Ormerod and that they intend to live in the property on completion. They have instructed their conveyancer that they would like to hold the property as tenants-in-common in equal shares.

HM Land Registry
Transfer of whole of registered title(s)

Any parts of the form that are not typed should be completed in black ink and in block capitals.

If you need more room than is provided for in a panel, and your software allows, you can expand any panel in the form. Alternatively use continuation sheet CS and attach it to this form.

For information on how HM Land Registry processes your personal information, see our <u>Personal Information Charter</u>.

Leave blank if not yet registered.	1 Title number(s) of the property: SK98765
Insert address including postcode (if any) or other description of the property, for example 'land adjoining 2 Acacia Avenue'.	2 Property: School House, The Green, Barnford, Berkshire BR5 6YH
Remember to date this deed with the day of completion, but not before it has been signed and witnessed.	3 Date:
Give full name(s) of **all** the persons transferring the property.	4 Transferor: Sophia Carol Hayward
Complete as appropriate where the transferor is a company.	<u>For UK incorporated companies/LLPs</u> Registered number of company or limited liability partnership including any prefix: <u>For overseas companies</u> (a) Territory of incorporation: (b) Registered number in the United Kingdom including any prefix:

Give full name(s) of **all** the persons to be shown as registered proprietors.

Complete as appropriate where the transferee is a company. Also, for an overseas company, unless an arrangement with HM Land Registry exists, lodge either a certificate in Form 7 in Schedule 3 to the Land Registration Rules 2003 or a certified copy of the constitution in English or Welsh, or other evidence permitted by rule 183 of the Land Registration Rules 2003.

Each transferee may give up to three addresses for service, one of which must be a postal address whether or not in the UK (including the postcode, if any). The others can be any combination of a postal address, a UK DX box number or an electronic address.

5	Transferee for entry in the register: Michael Ormerod and Jean Ormerod For UK incorporated companies/LLPs Registered number of company or limited liability partnership including any prefix: For overseas companies (a) Territory of incorporation: (b) Registered number in the United Kingdom including any prefix:
6	Transferee's intended address(es) for service for entry in the register: School House, The Green, Barnford, Berkshire BR5 6YH
7	The transferor transfers the property to the transferee

163

Place 'X' in the appropriate box. State the currency unit if other than sterling. If none of the boxes apply, insert an appropriate memorandum in panel 11.	**8 Consideration** ☒ The transferor has received from the transferee for the property the following sum (in words and figures): Five hundred and twenty five thousand pounds (£525,000) ☐ The transfer is not for money or anything that has a monetary value ☐ Insert other receipt as appropriate:
Place 'X' in any box that applies. Add any modifications.	**9 The transferor transfers with** ☒ full title guarantee ☐ limited title guarantee

Where the transferee is more than one person, place 'X' in the appropriate box.
 	
Complete as necessary.
 	
The registrar will enter a Form A restriction in the register *unless*:
– an 'X' is placed:
  – in the first box, or
  – in the third box and the details of the trust or of the trust instrument show that the transferees are to hold the property on trust for themselves alone as joint tenants, *or*
– it is clear from completion of a form
	10 Declaration of trust. The transferee is more than one person and
	
	☐ they are to hold the property on trust for themselves as joint tenants
	
	☒ they are to hold the property on trust for themselves as tenants in common in equal shares
	
	☐ they are to hold the property on trust:

JO lodged with this application that the transferees are to hold the property on trust for themselves alone as joint tenants.

Please refer to *Joint property ownership* and practice guide *24: private trusts of land* for further guidance. These are both available on the GOV.UK website.

Insert here any required or permitted statement, certificate or application and any agreed covenants, declarations and so on.

11   Additional provisions

The Transferees hereby covenant with the Transferor that the Transferees and the persons deriving title under them will at all times observe and perform the covenants and conditions contained or referred to in the charges register of title number SK98765 so far as they relate to the Property and will indemnify and keep the Transferor and her successors in title fully and effectively indemnified against all actions proceedings damages costs claims and expenses which may be suffered or incurred by the Transferor or her successors in title in respect of any future breach or non-observance or non-performance of those covenants and conditions.

The transferor must execute this transfer as a deed using the space opposite. If there is more than one transferor, all must execute. Forms of execution are given in Schedule 9 to the Land Registration Rules 2003. If the transfer contains transferee's covenants or declarations or contains an application by the transferee (such as for a restriction), it must also be executed by the transferee.

If there is more than one transferee and panel 10 has been completed, each transferee must also execute this transfer to comply with the requirements in section 53(1)(b) of the Law of Property Act 1925 relating to the declaration of a trust of land. Please refer to *Joint property ownership* and practice guide *24: private trusts of land* for further guidance.

Examples of the correct form of execution are set out in practice guide 8: execution of deeds. Execution as a deed usually means that a witness must also sign, and add their name and address.

Remember to date this deed in panel 3.

12	Execution

Signed and delivered as a deed
By the said Sophia Carol Hayward
In the presence of:

Witness (sign)..............................

Witness (print name) ....

Witness (address)...........................

Signed and delivered as a deed
By the said Michael Ormerod
In the presence of:

Witness (sign)..............................

Witness (print name) ....

Witness (address)...........................

Signed and delivered as a deed
By the said Jean Ormerod
In the presence of:

Witness (sign)..............................

Witness (print name) ....

Witness (address)...........................

WARNING

If you dishonestly enter information or make a statement that you know is, or might be, untrue or misleading, and intend by doing so to make a gain for yourself or another person, or to cause loss or the risk of loss to another person, you may commit the offence of fraud under section 1 of the Fraud Act 2006, the maximum penalty for which is 10 years' imprisonment or an unlimited fine, or both.

Failure to complete this form with proper care may result in a loss of protection under the Land Registration Act 2002 if, as a result, a mistake is made in the register.

Under section 66 of the Land Registration Act 2002 most documents (including this form) kept by the registrar relating to an application to the registrar or referred to in the register are open to public inspection and copying. If you believe a document contains prejudicial information, you may apply for that part of the document to be made exempt using Form EX1, under rule 136 of the Land Registration Rules 2003.

© Crown copyright (ref: LR/HO) 06/19

Completion Information and Undertakings (2019)

This is one of the Protocol forms. It will usually be sent by the buyer's conveyancer to the seller's conveyancer for completion by them and return before the completion date. The form contains some important information:

1. where the keys to the property will be left (often with the estate agent)

2. what documents will be handed over to the buyer's conveyancer on completion (this must include the signed transfer)

3. confirmation that the seller's conveyancer will adopt the Law Society's Code for Completion by Post (2019). This is an important set of procedures whereby the seller's conveyancer agrees to deal with the completion documents on behalf of the buyer's conveyancer on completion. It is another form which contains undertakings and therefore must be treated with respect. You will remember that this form was amended following the *Dreamvar* case to confirm that the seller's conveyancer confirms

that they act for the true owner of the property. The buyer's conveyancer can rely on this statement.

Practice Points

Many firms will insist that the seller's conveyancer provides replies to Completion Information and Undertakings prior to exchange or at the very least, that the seller's conveyancer will be adopting the Code for Completion by Post (2019) unamended. This is because the buyer's conveyancer wants the reassurance that they can rely on the seller's conveyancer having carried out appropriate AML and due diligence checks against their seller client. If the seller's conveyancer ever indicates that they wish to amend the Code for Completion by Post (2019), alert a qualified professional.

4. confirmation as to how much money is payable by the buyer on completion (often 90% of the purchase price, 10% having been paid on exchange). It also includes the bank account details of the client account for the seller's conveyancer. We have seen that sending bank account details by email represents a significant cybercrime risk. It is for this reason that as a risk management procedure, many conveyancers insist on receiving a hardcopy of this form and/or confirmation of the client account details at the beginning of the transaction

5. confirmation as to exactly which mortgages the seller's conveyancer will be paying off out of the sale proceeds on completion. This is one of the riskiest parts of the transaction for the seller's conveyancer. Completing this part of the form acts as an undertaking. The seller's conveyancer should include the name of the lender and the date of the charges as appearing on the charges register of title for the mortgages which they undertake to redeem out of the sale proceeds. This form should be checked and signed by a partner or suitably qualified fee earner.

Practice Points

It must be understood that completing this form is not just administration. As we have seen, adoption of the Code for

Completion by Post (2019) acts as confirmation by the seller's conveyancer that they act for the true owner of the property. It also contains a professionally binding undertaking regarding the payment of the mortgages. The significance of this is that even if the seller's conveyancer does not hold enough money to pay off the mortgage is on completion, they will be obliged to do so out of the firm's own money. It is for this reason that the seller's conveyancer should obtain an indicative redemption figure for all mortgages prior to exchange of contracts. This is an important part of the conveyancing jigsaw.

Link: https://www.lawsociety.org.uk/topics/property/transaction-forms

<u>Pre-completion searches</u>

The buyer's conveyancer must carry out pre-completion searches. These will usually be done just after exchange of contracts.

Practice Points

The two main searches are the bankruptcy search if there is a lender and the HMLR official search of the register with priority. If the seller is a limited company (for example, a developer on a new build), it will be necessary to carry out a company search. There will be different searches required if the title is unregistered and other checks to make if a Power of Attorney is used or if there is a probate sale.

Bankruptcy search

We have already seen that the buyer's conveyancer should do a bankruptcy search against the full name of all of the buyers prior to exchange of contracts. This search must be repeated before completion if the buyer is getting a mortgage. The purpose of the search is to check on behalf of the lender that there are no bankruptcy proceedings against the buyer.

Land registry search

This is an important surge and is a key part of risk management in any conveyancing transaction. You will remember from our fictitious register of title that there is a 'search from' date at the top of the register of title. This is the date which must appear in the search application. Note that there is a lender, the search must be done on behalf of the lender, as the name appears on the mortgage deed.

Practice Points

If there is no lender, that is, you have a cash buyer, the applicant for the HMLR search will be the full name of all buyers. However, if there is a lender, the applicant will be the name of the lender but note that this must be as the lender's name appears on the mortgage deed.

For example, Britannia is a trading name of The Co-operative Bank plc. You will do your search in the name of 'The Co-operative Bank plc'.

If purchasing all of the property in a title, the Official Search with priority: whole title will be carried out. This is known as the OS1 search.

Official copy of register of title **Title number SK98765** **Edition date 06.08.2019**

- **This official copy shows the entries on the register of title on 29 September 2021 at 10.34.10.**
- **This date must be quoted as the "search from date" in any official search application based on this copy.**
- The date at the beginning of an entry is the date on which the entry was made in the register.
- Issued on 06 September 2021.
- Under s.67 of the Land Registration Act 2002, this copy is admissible in evidence to the same extent as the original.
- This title is dealt with by Land Registry Weymouth Office.

The purpose of the official search with priority is twofold:

1. it acts as a means of updating the register since the search from date meaning that if any other entries have been added onto the seller's title since that day, these will be revealed by the search result. This means that if, for example, the seller has added a

further mortgage to the charges register, the buyer's conveyancer will be able to demand an undertaking to redeem it out of the sale proceeds on completion

2. it confers a 30-working day priority period from the date of the search result. The purpose of this priority period is to give the buyers conveyancer 30 working days within which to complete the transaction and make the application for registration of the buyer's purchase. The priority period protects the buyer in that if a third-party tries to register an entry against the seller's title during that time, that application will be held in abeyance thus giving the buyer's conveyancer time to make the registration application

Practice Points

It is essential that the expiry of the priority period is diarised, whether on the buyer's file, a case management system or a paper diary. It is also essential to ensure that the application for registration to HMLR is made within this priority period. If it is not, any application which is being held in abeyance will be registered upon expiry of the priority period.

An important misconception is that the priority period can be extended. It cannot. If you think that you are not going to be able to make the HMLR application within the priority period, you should carry out another priority search. This gives a new priority period but does not extend the first one.

Practice Points

The above searches used to be routinely carried out by completing paper forms. However, the vast majority of conveyancing firms will now carry out these searches using the HMLR portal. HMLR has an excellent range of 'how to' guides. See links below

https://www.gov.uk/guidance/land-registry-portal-official-search-of-whole-with-priority

https://www.gov.uk/guidance/land-registry-portal-how-to-make-a-bankruptcy-search

Obtaining the funds to complete

As we have seen, the buyer's conveyancer will send a completion statement to their buyer client which will often show a sum of money due from the buyer to enable completion to proceed. The conveyancer must ensure that their buyer client pays any money due well in advance of completion to ensure that the conveyancer holds cleared funds on the day of completion.

If the buyer is getting a mortgage, the conveyancer must submit a standard form to the lender called a Certificate of Title. Most lenders require between 5 and 7 working days' notice between receipt of the Certificate of Title and release of the mortgage advance to the conveyancer's client account.

The Certificate of Title acts as a request for the drawdown of the mortgage advance but also acts as confirmation from the conveyancing firm that the title to the property is 'good and marketable'.

Practice Points

You should check the terms of the mortgage offer carefully to establish how many days' notice the particular lender requires to release the funds. Lenders will generally not guarantee to release the mortgage advance to the conveyancer on the morning of drawdown of the loan. Accordingly, it is becoming standard practice for the conveyancer to request release of the mortgage advance the day before completion to ensure that no delay is incurred in this regard. Indeed, many lenders now release the funds the day before as a matter of course.

There are a number of ways to submit the Certificate of Title to the lender. Many now use an electronic portal such as Lender Exchange, others will require the form to be faxed to them some even require a hard copy to be put in the post. You should check the requirements of the particular lender before exchange of contracts.

Stage of the conveyancing process

SELLER	BUYER
COMPLETION STAGE OF THE TRANSACTION	
This is the moving date that was agreed in the contract on exchange	
This is the date that the buyer's conveyancer sends the balance of the purchase money in return for the title to the property which passes from the seller to the buyer in the transfer document	
Completion date	Completion date Send completion money to the seller's conveyancer via bank transfer **RISK!** What steps are taken to check where the completion money is being sent to?
Confirm receipt of completion money Inform buyer's conveyancer Inform seller client Contact estate agent to confirm that keys can be 'released' to the buyer	

The day of completion

The completion date is agreed between seller and buyer and is inserted into the contract on exchange of contracts. We have seen the steps that the conveyancers must take to prepare for completion. On the day of completion, the buyer's conveyancer will usually arrange with their accounts department that a telegraphic transfer of the purchase money is sent to the client account of the conveyancing firm acting for the seller.

Once the purchase money is received by the seller's conveyancer, they will:

- contact the buyer's conveyancer to confirm receipt of the funds and confirm completion
- contact their seller client to confirm completion
- contact the estate agent (if any) to confirm that the keys can be released to the buyer

- pay off the seller's mortgage by telegraphic transfer in accordance with the undertaking given before completion
- insert the completion date by hand into the transfer and send the original transfer plus any other relevant documents (for example, planning permissions or guarantees) to the buyer's conveyancer (the seller's conveyancer should keep a certified copy of the signed, dated transfer for their file incase the original goes astray)
- if the contract contained a clause obliging the seller to obtain indemnity insurance, this should be applied for and the policy sent to the buyer's conveyancer when received
- pay any sale proceeds due to the seller
- the seller has a related purchase transaction the net sale proceeds should be transferred to the firm's purchase ledger to enable the purchase to complete

Practice Points

We have seen that cybercrime is a significant conveyancing risk. As an additional risk management procedure, many conveyancing firms will contact the seller's conveyancer on the day of completion to reaffirm the client account details to which the purchase money is to be sent and will cross check to ensure that this is the same as the information provided on the Completion Information and Undertakings Form. Similar checks may be made when sending funds to a lender to redeem the seller's mortgage or sending the net sale proceeds to the seller.

Stage of the conveyancing process

SELLER	BUYER
POST COMPLETION STAGE OF THE TRANSACTION	
The seller and the buyer have moved and are generally no longer interested in their conveyancer!	
This is the stage of the transaction where some important work has to be done by the conveyancers acting for the seller and the buyer	
Send transfer and any other documents to buyer's conveyancer	Pay SDLT (if any) within 14 days of completion
Redeem mortgage/s if any	
Pay estate agent's account, if approved by the seller	
Send evidence of removal of mortgage/s if any to buyer's conveyancer and obtain release from undertaking given on completion	Register title (and mortgage, if any) within priority period of OS1 search **RISK!** It is vital for the buyer's conveyancer to submit the HMLR in time
	Check completed registration for accuracy
Close file	Close file

Post-completion

Both sets of conveyancers have important work to do after completion has taken place. Generally, their clients are not interested at this stage. The sale and purchase have completed, the buyers have moved in and they are generally not interested in work to be done by the conveyancers. However, this represents a risky part of the transaction and should not be seen by any firm as simply administrative tasks.

Seller's conveyancer

If the seller has used an estate agent, the latter will usually expect to be paid by the conveyancer out of the sale proceeds. This is generally acceptable and the seller's conveyancer will include the estate agents' fees on the completion statement. However, it is important to understand that the seller must authorise their conveyancer to pay the estate agent on completion. The invoice should also be made out to the seller and not to the conveyancing firm.

Once the seller's conveyancer has paid off the seller's mortgage if any, they will send evidence of removal of the charge from the charges register of title to the buyer's conveyancer and should request a release from the undertaking given on completion.

If not done already, they will render their bill. When all of the above tasks are concluded and balances on the accounts ledgers are zero, the file can be closed.

Buyer's conveyancer

There are some very important timeframes to be met after completion of a purchase. Failure to meet these deadlines could result in a negligence claim being brought against the firm and this therefore one of the riskiest parts of the transaction.

Stamp Duty Land Tax (SDLT)

We have seen that SDLT is payable in relation to most purchase transactions. This is a self-assessment tax meaning that the conveyancing firm must rely on the information provided by their buyer as to the amount of SDLT payable. Firms will generally ask their buyer client to sign a form SDLT1 in advance of completion. This form contains details of the transaction, the property, the parties and the purchase price to ensure that the correct declaration is made to HMRC and the correct tax is paid. Link:

https://www.gov.uk/government/publications/sdlt-guide-for-completing-paper-sdlt1-return/guide-for-completing-paper-sdlt1-returns

The SDLT1 and any tax payable must be submitted to HMRC within 14 days of the completion date. Failure to do so will result in a penalty and interest being payable.

Once the return is submitted, HMRC will issue a certificate called SDLT5. This certificate must be sent with the HMLR application for registration (see below).

Practice Points

Most firms will use HMRC's SDLT online calculator to work out the amount of tax payable. Link:

https://www.tax.service.gov.uk/calculate-stamp-duty-land-tax/#/intro

Most firms will also submit the SDLT1 form to HMRC online although it is possible to send a hard copy of the form in the post. Link:

https://www.gov.uk/guidance/stamp-duty-land-tax-online-and-paper-returns

HMLR application

The buyer's conveyancer must make the application to HMLR to register the transfer of ownership from the seller to the buyer within the 30-working day OS1 priority period.

If the buyer has a mortgage, this should also be registered at the same time. If the title is registered, a former AP1 will be used. A typical application for registration where the seller had a mortgage that has been redeemed and a buyer took out a new mortgage involves submitting the following documents to HMLR:

- Completed from AP1
- Evidence of removal of the seller's mortgage
- The dated TR1
- The mortgage deed signed by the buyer and dated with the date of completion
- Form SDLT5

If a registration is submitted after the expiry of the priority period and a third-party has an application to make a registration against the seller's title being held in abeyance, this will be added to the title (if valid) as soon as the priority period expires. This means that the buyer will take the property subject to this additional entry which has been added to the seller's title. If this is a further mortgage or an adverse entry, the buyer's conveyancer will probably be negligent.

Land law links

Legal title to the property passes from the seller (transferor) to the buyer (transferee) upon registration.

Practice Points

Most firms will use the HMLR portal to make their applications for registration. See Chapter 9 for future developments in this area.

Once the registration is complete, the buyer's conveyancer should first check that the registration has been completed correctly – if there are any errors or discrepancies these should be addressed with HMLR immediately. They should then check the lender's requirements to establish whether the lender requires a copy of the title or any documents. They should also check the requirements of their buyer client in relation to any documents.

A conveyancer should bring the HMLR Property Alert service to the attention of their buyer. This is a free service designed to help mitigate property fraud. A registered proprietor can create a Property Alert account and can monitor up to 10 properties. If there are activities on the registers of the title is, HMLR will issue an email alert. Link:

https://www.gov.uk/guidance/property-alert

Buyers should also be reminded to keep their address for service on the proprietorship register up-to-date.

If not done already, they will render their bill. When all of the above tasks are concluded and balances on the accounts ledgers are zero, the file can be closed.

CHAPTER NINE
FUTURE DEVELOPMENTS

There are many areas of conveyancing which are fast developing. An example is in relation to leasehold properties but this is outside the scope of this Practical Guide. This Chapter contains a short summary of some of the most significant changes in conveyancing practice. You will note that they relate to HMLR initiatives. All conveyancers should consider subscribing to the HMLR regular updates and blogs because these are the communication channels through which HMLR tend to announce changes.

Local land charges

We have seen that formation relating to local land charges forms part of the pre-contract local search. Form LLC1 is one part of the local search application. The information to respond to the LLC1 enquiries has until recently been held by local authorities. However, a programme of transferring this information to HMLR has started.

The common obligations protected as local land charges include:

- planning permissions (these form the majority of charges)

- listed buildings

- conservation areas

- tree preservation orders

- improvement and renovation grants

- smoke control zone conditions

- light obstruction notice conditions

A number of local authorities have already transferred their data to HMLR meaning that the LLC1 information must now be obtained from HMLR. Eventually, it is intended that all local authorities transfer their information to HMLR. In practice, this will probably have little day-today impact on conveyancers because the commercial search companies which most conveyancers use will manage this issue. Once a local authority's local land charges data has been transferred to HMLR, it will no longer be possible to obtain LLC1 search results from that local authority.

Note, however, that local authorities will continue to provide replies to Con29 enquiries

More information can be found in HMLR PG79.

Electronic signatures

HMLR will now accept for registration deeds which have been signed electronically. PG82 sets out HMLR's specific requirements in this regard.

Law Brief Publishing have published a book considering the issues for conveyancers that this significant change to HMLR practice raises: '*A Practical Guide to Document Signing and Electronic Signatures for Conveyancers*'.

Digital registration

HMLR portal users can use the Digital Registration Service to submit HMLR applications online. This replaces the electronic Document Registration Service (e-DRS).

Digital Registration Service makes it easier to submit applications and reduce common errors by:

- automatically working out the fees

- comparing information with the Land Register as you enter it to check for errors

- providing guidance and prompts on screen to remind you to add the required evidence

- automatically populating some fields based on data already entered, or from the Land Register

- prompting you if more information or supporting evidence is required to support your application

- allowing you to save a partially completed application, and return to it within 90 calendar days to submit

HMLR has said:

> 'A digital application process, based on data rather than traditional paper-based methods, is fundamental to transforming the way we register land and ultimately will play a vital role in improving the end-to-end conveyancing journey. Not only does it offer the immediate benefits of quicker processing times and fewer errors, but it opens the opportunity for further innovation in the future.'

From November 2022, HMLR will no longer accept scanned or PDF copies of AP1s for changes to existing titles via the HMLR portal.

Digital identity

You can see that the drive to digitisation is central to HMLR's strategy. HMLR has introduced its Digital Identity standard which is an alternative standard for checking identity that can be applied immediately. The enhanced level of check is defined by reference to a set of requirements which involve biometric and cryptographic checking of identity and verification. A conveyancer who adopts this approach will have fulfilled their obligation to take reasonable steps in relation to the requirement to verify their client's identity. This means that if a conveyancer carries out the steps described in the standard, HMLR will not pursue any recourse claim against the conveyancer resulting from the registration of a fraudulent transaction on the grounds that identity checks were inadequate.

PG 81 contains more information.

CHAPTER TEN
RISKS SUMMARY

Conveyancing is fraught with risk and firms are battling all the time to manage and mitigate these risks. We have mentioned many of the risks throughout this Practical Guide, which are summarised below.

Chapter 1 – Conveyacing, land law and transaction overview

A valid contract simply needs to be signed by or on behalf of the parties to it – contrast this with the signing requirements for a deed

Title to land can only be transferred by deed (s52 LPA 1925) which is a special type of document which complies with certain statutory requirements. To be a valid deed the document must be:

- **in writing**
- **intended on the face of it to be a deed** (the document usually describes itself as a deed)
- **validly executed** (that is, signed).

Protecting a buyer if there is a behind the scenes beneficial interest

> **One registered proprietor and no Form A restriction** – a buyer can buy from the sole registered proprietor
>
> **Two registered proprietors and a Form A restriction** – a buyer can buy from the 2 registered proprietors. Although the restriction denotes a behind-the-scenes beneficial interest, we already have the 2 trustees in place to overreach.
>
> **One registered proprietor and a Form A restriction** – the buyer must be careful! A buyer must ensure that a second trustee is appointed to overreach the beneficial interest

You must be able to recognise when a second trustee should be appointed. If you do not have experience of dealing with this aspect, it is vital to ensure that a qualified professional amends the contract and approves the transfer document as required to ensure that there are no problems after completion.

Chapter 2 – Regulation, professional conduct and client care

Undertakings

- an undertaking can be given orally
- an undertaking can be given by anyone in a law firm, it does not have to be given by a qualified professional
- the word 'undertaking' does not need to be used for a statement to be construed as such
- best practice demands that undertakings are only given and signed by qualified professionals or someone with sufficient training

Confidentiality

- solicitors and licensed conveyancers are obliged to keep client matters confidential and, crucially, to ensure that everyone working in the firm does so

Conflicts of interest

- if a conflict-of-interest arises during a transaction or there is a significant risk of a conflict arising, a solicitor must cease continuing to act for both clients and must send them elsewhere. Thus, if we think that there might be a significant risk of a conflict-of-interest arising between two or more clients, we should not act in the first place

Awareness and ask!

- the key to all conduct issues is awareness. You should always think about conduct issues and, before taking any steps such as sending a document or telling someone that you will do something, take time out to ask a qualified professional
- if you are in any doubt as to whether you can deal with a party or give information, you should always check with your client first. Simply contact your client and seek their instructions. In

terms of confidentiality, once the genie is out of the bottle, it cannot be put back

Acting for seller and buyer in the same transaction

- SRA regulated law firms should not be doing this is as a matter of course
- The CLC's position is different in that their Conflicts of Interest Code does allow the same conveyancing firm to act for the seller and the buyer in the same conveyancing transaction provided certain conditions are met

Client care issues

At the start of the retainer, clients must be told about:

- their right to complain. If a firm does not resolve a client's complaint within 8 weeks, they can complain to the Legal Ombudsman
- the work to be done on the file
- the legal fees, vat and disbursements (outgoings)
- if the legal fees are not shown as being subject to vat, the fees will be deemed to include vat

Chapter 3 – Due diligence and money

Accounts Rules

- money belonging to clients must be kept separate from money belonging to the firm or business
- client money and business money must never be mixed
- client account is never permitted to become overdrawn
- client money must be cleared through the banking system before it can be used. The reason for this is that it is a breach of the Accounts Rules to allow money belonging to one client to be inadvertently used for the purposes of another

Anti-Money Laundering (AML)

- To enable firms to take a risk-based approach to the risk of money-laundering and terrorist financing, the firm should have:

  client risk assessments which should identify and assess the money laundering and terrorist financing risks identified at individual client levels; and

  matter risk assessments which should be carried out on each new matter for a client (particularly where risks are new or non-repetitive)

- Conveyancers should be aware of their firm's risk assessment procedures and the firm's requirements regarding issues such as identification and source of funds/wealth

Money laundering warning signs

- a buyer who is purchasing with cash (that is, not taking out any mortgage financing to fund the purchase)
- payments coming into the conveyancing firm from a number of different individuals or sources
- money being paid into the conveyancing firm from a party other than the client of the firm
- multiple owners of a property
- a foreign element
- sudden or unexplained changes in ownership of property
- an unusual sale price
- an unwillingness by the client to prove identity
- a client who is anxious to pay over funds for a prospective transaction, before it is requested, unless there is a justifiable reason. A simple way to launder money is to pay money to a conveyancer ostensibly being a large deposit for a house purchase or some other transaction, which is quickly cancelled. The client therefore asks for their money back from the conveyancer and the illegal money has been 'cleaned' through the firm's client account

- a situation where money is paid direct between the seller and buyer and not via the conveyancing firms

Know Your Client

This involves a combination of factors including:

- the need for the firm to carry out appropriate identification and verification procedures
- the need for the firm to verify 'beneficial owners' of a client
- the need for the firm to obtain information on the purpose of the client's business relationship with the firm and the purpose of the underlying transaction

Do not underestimate the importance of basic questions to a conveyancing client such as:

'Why are you selling this property?'

'Why are you buying this property?'

'What is the purpose of this transaction?'

Identifying the client

Law firms need to carry out identification checks to comply with AML obligations and obligations imposed by the Lender's Handbook

- some firms will require clients to attend the office to produce originals of the documents in lists A and B in the Lender's Handbook for photocopying and handing back to the client
- some firms will require clients to personally attend with their own documents and will not accept identification documents produced by anyone else (for example, a spouse of the client
- many firms will subscribe to additional electronic checks which will be carried out against the name of all clients instructing the firm
- central to any electronic checks is ensuring that the correct name is searched against

Source of funds and source of wealth

Consider the level of risk:

- Low risk – property funded from proceeds of sale, and/or mortgage
- Medium risk – property funded form proceeds of sale, and/or mortgage and savings
- High risk – purchases being funded from substantial private funds; 3rd party funding; complicated funding arrangements; corporate or overseas funding

- Source of funds seeks to establish where is the client's money now, which will typically be in a bank account in the client's name
- Source of wealth seeks to establish where that money came from.
- Each conveyancing firm will set out in its PCPs what evidence is acceptable to establish source of wealth. This can be a complex financial task/review and in the event that a conveyancer feels unsure as to how to assess any evidence produced by the client, they should refer to an immediate superior and/or the firm's MLRO

What if the funds are coming from a third-party?

- The most obvious example of this is a 'gifted deposit' in a conveyancing transaction, for example, parents are making a gift of some money to the firm's client to assist with a purchase
- Many conveyancing firms will have additional requirements in their PCPs to deal with funds coming from a third-party including obtaining identification documents for that third-party
- A conveyancing firm should avoid acting for the third-party due to the significant risk of a conflict-of-interest arising

What if the funds are coming from abroad?

- If the client provides evidence that any money is coming from a non-UK based bank account, the firm should adopt a more stringent approach to source of funds and source of wealth

- Conveyancers should understand their firm's requirements in relation to assets such as bitcoin and crypto currency
- If it is evident from the information provided by the client that their money is anywhere other than in a UK based bank account, the conveyancer should make further enquiries or ask a qualified professional or the firm's Money Laundering Reporting Officer before confirming the retainer or accepting money into client account

What if the client wants you to send money abroad?

- Many conveyancing firms have a straightforward requirement that any money being sent by the firm to the client (for example, the net sale proceeds on completion of a sale transaction) must be sent to a UK based bank account in the name of the client

Client account must not be used as a banking facility

- Law firms should not allow their client account to be used as a banking facility for their clients
- Firms should always ask themselves why they are being asked to make a payment or why the client cannot make all received payment directly themselves

Money laundering myths

- If a client's money is already in a UK based bank account it must be 'clean' and the firm does not need to check it – myth! Conveyancing firms cannot assume that UK banks check the source of deposits. The Financial Conduct Authority fined HSBC Bank plc £63.9m for *'failings in its anti-money laundering processes'*. (Source: www.fca.org.uk, Dec 2021)
- Money-laundering must involve an international element – myth! Money-laundering can involve seemingly mundane processes such as not paying tax to HMRC or defrauding money from an employer
- Money-laundering could not happen to our firm, we are a local High Street firm – myth! Fraudsters will target smaller, local

firms perhaps assuming that their AML procedures are not as robust

- A conveyancing firm can rely on identification documents certified by another professional organisation – myth! It is up to each firm to determine the level of risk that it is prepared to take but a firm will not automatically be protected if documents certified by another organisation subsequently turn out to be fraudulent

- A conveyancing firm only has to check the client's identity; there is no obligation to ask about the source of funds – myth! As we have seen above, enquiring as to source of funds and source of wealth is a central part of AML due diligence

- A conveyancing firm must prove that a client's money is clean – myth! A conveyancing firm is required to consider whether the source of funds and wealth is consistent with the risk profile of the client, the retainer and their business

There are a number of do's and don'ts which will help to mitigate the risk of the firm being a victim of money-laundering:

- understand your firm's PCPs in relation to these matters
- understand whether you are permitted to carry out any work on a client file before all of the AML, identification and due diligence procedures are satisfactorily concluded
- if a firm uses an electronic third-party verification tool, ensure that it is used properly and correctly on every client. The LSAG Guidance points out a basic, but important risk here, that of human error, it is *sensitive to human error, and mistakes of data input can lead to the incorrect individual being checked*' (para 7.3)
- under no circumstances should any suspicions or concerns be shared with the client – this could amount to 'tipping off' which would alert the client to the firm's suspicions and which in itself is an offence
- know who to ask in the event of a question/problem – either go to an immediate superior or the firm's MLRO
- act immediately – share concerns with the appropriate person in the firm at the earliest possible opportunity

- do not share any suspicions or concerns with anyone outside the firm, whether a partner/ spouse of the client, estate agent, mortgage broker or other conveyancer

- do not attempt to report any concern – if a conveyancer has any questions about a client's identification documents, source of funds/wealth or any other matter, this should be reported to the MLRO. It is the role of the MLRO to make a 'Suspicious Activity Report' (SAR) to the National Crime Agency (NCA) if there is an ongoing concern – the individual conveyancer should not do this

- do not see identification, verification and risk assessment as a one-off task to be completed at the beginning of a transaction. It is an ongoing responsibility throughout the life of a matter

- ensure that all steps taken and decisions made in relation to these matters are properly noted on the file

- a conveyancing firm is not obliged to take on a client or their transaction, so if a firm has a continued suspicion about a client, they could decline to act

- AML, identification and due diligence procedures are not just 'administration'. They are an integral part of the conveyancing process which assist in protecting the firm from fraud and money laundering

- AML, identification and due diligence procedures are everyone's job!

- if in doubt – ask! In the majority of cases, a suspicion about a client's activities will not result in a finding of money laundering but conveyancers must be encouraged to trust their instincts and share concerns with the appropriate person in the firm

Seller fraud

Warning signs:

- the only contact details for the client being a mobile member and/or email address

- where a firm is instructed by more than one person but meets only one party to a transaction

- obvious typographical errors or alterations in documents presented as utility bills (for identification purposes)
- the client being unable or unwilling to provide documentation linking them to the address
- changes to the clients contact details or bank account to which the sale proceeds are to be sent

Impersonation of a law firm and identity theft

Steps that conveyancing firms can take to mitigate the risk of this type of fraud including:

- using an electronic checking service to confirm that the law firm or office exists
- checking a firm's website to ensure that a branch office exists
- insisting on receiving at least some communication from the firm via the post as opposed to all correspondence being by email
- telephoning the senior partner of the firm to ensure that a branch office exists
- checking that the law firm on the other side is on record with, for example, the SRA, CLC or other legal regulatory body is practising at the address provided (note that this is a specific requirement in section 3 (safeguards) of the Lender's Handbook)
- checking with the SRA, CLC or other legal regulatory body that the that the fee earner dealing with the transaction is a recognised, regulated individual (e.g., by using the Law Society's 'Find a Solicitor' service)

Cyber threats

Common procedures which conveyancing firms put in place to minimise the risk of cybercrime are:

- wording on all email footers indicating that the firm's bank account details will not change
- a procedure to verify the recipient and check bank account details of the recipient every time a telegraphic transfer is sent out (this is particular important on completion

- a policy that the firms bank account details will not be sent to anyone outside the firm by email (even as a PDF attachment)
- training staff to be cautious about emails received that seem unusual or have poor spelling and grammar
- training staff to avoid opening unsolicited emails with links and attachments
- ensuring that staff know whom to contact in the event that a suspicious communication is received or, worse, a problem is identified or a suspicious link is opened

Examples of red flags in conveyancing

- a cash transaction
- the client not being local to your firm and not providing a reasonable explanation as to why they have chosen your firm
- an empty property (for example because the owner has died)
- a high value property
- a property with no mortgage
- a property that is let (tenanted)
- foreign element (e.g. client is abroad or they want the money sent abroad)
- unexplained urgency
- not meeting the client face to face
- seller's address not the same as the property being sold

Chapter 4 – Title to land

- If the buyer's conveyancer has any questions or concerns about the seller's title, these will be raised as part of the buyers 'pre-contract enquiries'. The buyer's conveyancer should not exchange contracts until all of these enquiries and matters of title have been answered to their satisfaction.
- It is imperative that a bundle of unregistered title deeds is stored safely in the firm's strongroom and the deeds must not be released to the buyer's conveyancer until such time as completion has taken place

- If you see possessory title when acting for a buyer or lender, always raise it with a qualified practitioner. Exchange of contracts should not take place until this has been satisfactorily addressed

- Always ensure that the contract contains the correct estate in land and the exact address as per the property register

- Anything other than title absolute should be raised as a pre-contract enquiry with the seller's conveyancer

- A conveyancer acting for a buyer should seek confirmation in the pre-contract enquiries that this certificate will be handed over on completion

- A restriction is a danger for a buyer's conveyancer. A restriction could mean that the buyer's registration cannot be concluded after completion of the buyer's purchase. A conveyancer should always look very carefully at the terms of a restriction and, if necessary, raise a pre-contract enquiry. It is essential for a buyer's conveyancer to be satisfied, prior to exchange of contracts, that a restriction can be complied with after completion or that the conveyancer can obtain the necessary consent or certificate after completion

- The overriding interest of most risk and concern to a buyer in a residential conveyancing transaction is the person who is in actual occupation of the property who has an interest in the land but, crucially, does not appear on the register of title

- If the buyer's conveyancer is in any doubt, they should not advise their buyer to exchange contracts until the position relating to a non-owning occupier is resolved

- The seller's conveyancer should not also act for a non-owning occupier. They should send the contract to the occupier for signature and return but also tell the occupier to obtain their own independent legal advice if they are in any doubt as to their position

Chapter 5 – Taking instructions and indemnity insurance

Taking instructions on a sale

- As a matter of professional conduct, a conveyancer must ensure that they take instructions from all sellers of a property

- It is important to carry out a conflict check when full details of the buyer are known
- If the seller does not live at the property being sold, the conveyancer must establish whether the property is currently empty (vacant) or whether someone else lives in the property
- The seller's conveyancer must also be satisfied that the seller is the true owner of the property
- If a seller has not lived in a property for the entire period of their ownership, they may be liable to pay Capital Gains Tax (CGT) on the sale proceeds on completion. This is not something which a conveyancer should advise about in detail because we are lawyers not accountants. The conveyancer should advise the seller to obtain detailed accountancy advice prior to exchange of contracts if there is a possibility that CGT might be payable on the sale proceeds
- A non-owning occupier can cause a problem for a buyer. The buyer's conveyancer will want to ensure that overreaching takes place, if relevant, and that any non-owning occupier signs the contract as evidence of their intention to move out of the property on completion
- The seller's conveyancer will be required to give an undertaking to redeem (pay off) all mortgages appearing on the seller's charges register
- An essential part of the risk management process for the seller's conveyancer is to write to all lenders to obtain indicative redemption figures on all registered charges prior to exchange of contracts
- If the seller wants the sale proceeds to be sent to a bank account, the conveyancer will usually ask for details of the bank account to which the sale proceeds are to be sent at an early stage in the transaction. This will usually be a UK based bank account in the name of the seller
- Is the sale dependent on a related purchase transaction?
- Obtaining the seller's signatures is an important part of the due diligence and identification processes

- Request consent to deal with others who might crop up – confidentiality

Taking instructions on a purchase

- The purchase price will be inserted in the contract and should appear in the mortgage offer if a mortgage is needed
- If the buyer agrees to purchase any additional items from the seller, the figure should be inserted in the contract and a list of the items included as an extra special condition
- It is important to carry out a conflict check when full details of the seller are known
- Even if the buyer has a related sale and/or needs a mortgage, they are likely to be contributing some of their own money to the purchase. The importance of source of funds and source of wealth checks from the point of view of AML and Lender's Handbook requirements
- If there is a gifted deposit, source of funds and source of wealth checks must be done and avoiding conflicts of interest must be considered
- Is the purchase dependent on a related sale transaction?
- Many conveyancers will carry out a bankruptcy search against their buyer client at the beginning of the transaction to check for any bankruptcy proceedings

Indemnity insurance

- Indemnity insurance is hardly ever a 'solution' in that it does not put the technical, legal problem which has arisen right
- No enquiry must be made of any person or organisation in the event that a problem arises. All conveyancers must understand that they should not make contact with anyone in the event that indemnity insurance might be needed. Furthermore, they should advise their clients not to make any such contact
- A copy of the required indemnity insurance policy should be attached to the contract, along with a draft statutory declaration or a statement of truth as to facts, if required

- If the seller will not pay for the policy, the buyer's conveyancer should consider advising their client to pay for the required indemnity insurance particularly if they have a lender involved

- The more recent the defect, the more expensive and indemnity insurance policy is likely to be, if one is available at all

- A conveyancer must not accept indemnity insurance on a purchase if they are unsure as to the terms of policy

- If there is a lender involved, it may also be necessary to check the Lenders Handbook (section 9) to establish whether the lender will accept indemnity insurance in the particular situation

- Request consent to deal with others who might crop up – confidentiality

Chapter 6 – Progressing a sale transaction

- CQS accredited firms who are obliged to use the Protocol should not include a large number of additional provisions or amendments to the special conditions as part of their standard contract

- The contract for the sale of land must be in writing (s2 1989 Act)

- If the seller has a mortgage registered over the property, their conveyancer should obtain an indicative redemption figure early in the transaction and certainly prior to exchange of contracts to ensure that the sale price is sufficient to cover costs and mortgages

- A buyer is entitled to rely on the seller's answers to the Property Information Form and pre-contract enquiries. If a buyer relies on answers which subsequently turn out to be incorrect, they may be able to sue the seller for misrepresentation after completion

- The seller's conveyancer should not forward emails from their client to any other party as this would be a breach of the firm's duty of confidentiality to their seller client

Chapter 7 – Progressing a purchase transaction

Pre-contract searches

- The LSAG Guidance states that firms can permit funds to be deposited in their client account if they are for fees and disbursements. So can ask a buyer client for money on account of searches before concluding the identification and AML due diligence procedures however, receiving any money into client account before conclusion of the due diligence can present a risk

- Conveyancing firms often advise buyer clients to take detailed accountancy advice prior to exchange of contracts if the SDLT position is not straightforward

- The buyer is not entitled to rely on a mortgage valuation report, even though they have paid for it

- Conveyancing lawyers are not surveyors and must avoid commenting or advising on a survey result if a buyer provides it

- An agreed allowance should be reported to any mortgage lender

- Conveyancers should be wary of a potential conflict-of-interest between buyers if they cannot agree how the beneficial interest will be held

- It is essential for the conveyancer to send the plan of the property to their buyer client prior to submitting the searches to seek the buyer's confirmation that the plan is correct and represents the full extent of the property being purchased

- An important limitation of the local search is that it only searches against the relevant property address

- The conveyancer must make it clear to the buyer that they are not qualified to interpret the environmental search result

- There is no 'magic' to raising enquiries but it is important to ensure that any enquiry is well drafted and specific, to elicit a meaningful response

- CQS accredited firms should not raise indiscriminate pre-contract enquiries

- A significant risk in relation to a purchase is to ensure that all pre-contract enquiries have been raised but, importantly, that they have also been properly answered. A key part of the skill of the conveyancer is to recognise when an answer or solution is acceptable. If you are in any doubt as to this, you should refer the matter to a qualified conveyancer or more experienced colleague. Under no circumstances should the transaction proceed to exchange of contracts until all such results have been received and pre-contract enquiries have been comprehensively answered

Financing a purchase

- A conveyancer must not give specific financial advice about a particular lender or mortgage product

- A solicitor or licensed conveyancer can tell a client what entering into the mortgage agreement means and the consequences of default but they cannot tell the client whether or not it is a good deal or recommend an alternative

- If a conveyancer acting for a lender discovers an issue about the property which is adverse, the conveyancer is under a duty to report such matters to the lender. A key risk for conveyancers is that they receive an unhelpful or fairly meaningless response from the lender. Best practice demands that conveyancers obtain authority to proceed from the lender in writing and that they do not rely on a telephone conversation in this regard.

- When reporting matters to a lender, the conveyancer must be aware of the possibility of a conflict-of-interest arising between the lender and the buyer.

- A conveyancer owes a duty of confidentiality to their buyer so they should ensure that they have the buyer's consent to notify the lender of any relevant issues prior to making contact with the lender.

- Most lenders require the conveyancer to submit the Certificate of Title at least 5 or 7 working days prior to the completion date. This is significant because if the conveyancer gives less notice than the lender requires, the conveyancer might not receive the mortgage advance in time for completion. This will put their buyer client in breach of contract.

- The Handbook requires the conveyancing firm to have the SDLT and HMLR fees in its client account prior to using the mortgage advance on the day of completion

Chapter 8 – Exchange to post completion

- It is important to ensure that the specifics relating to the property are brought to the client's attention and the client must understand what they have been told
- The conveyancer should not offer an opinion. The conveyancer should advise on what they have found out and explain the risks in language their client can understand and invite the client to instruct them as to whether or not the client wants to proceed

Exchange

- It is essential for a conveyancer to obtain their client's irrevocable authority to proceed to exchange of contracts, ideally in writing
- An inexperienced conveyancer should never be pressurised into exchanging
- If the client is willing to effectively 'break the chain' and go ahead on their sale without tying in their purchase, their conveyancer must obtain written instructions from their client confirming that they are willing to do this
- All of the formulae require the conveyancers to make a written memorandum of exchange of contracts to be placed on the file
- Use of all of the formulae involved implied undertakings which is another reason exchange is risky and must be carried out by someone with suitable experience
- Holding the deposit 'to order' is risky for the buyer's conveyancer because they might not actually hold any money in their client account but is simply relying on a similar undertaking given on their related sale
- Ensure that the agreed date of completion is properly diarised whether on a case management system, paper diary or the file

Preparing for completion

- It is essential for the seller's conveyancer to ensure that their seller client has signed the transfer in readiness for completion
- Sending bank account details by email represents a significant cybercrime risk. It is for this reason that as a risk management

procedure, many conveyancers insist on receiving a hardcopy of the Completion Information and Undertakings form and/or confirmation of the client account details at the beginning of the transaction

- Question 5 – Completion Information and Undertakings form – Completing this part of the form acts as an undertaking. The seller's conveyancer should include the name of the lender and the date of the charges as appearing on the charges register of title for the mortgages which they undertake to redeem out of the sale proceeds. This form should be checked and signed by a partner or suitably qualified fee earner

Pre-completion searches

- It is essential that the expiry of the priority period on the OS1 search is diarised, whether on the buyer's file, a case management system or a paper diary

Funds

- The conveyancer must ensure that their buyer client pays any money due well in advance of completion and that any mortgage advance is received in time to ensure that the conveyancer holds cleared funds on the day of completion

The day of completion

- We have seen that cybercrime is a significant conveyancing risk. As an additional risk management procedure, many conveyancing firms will contact the parties to whom money is going to be sent to verify account details

Post-completion

- The SDLT1 and any tax payable must be submitted to HMRC within 14 days of the completion date. Failure to do so will result in a penalty and interest being payable
- The buyer's conveyancer must make the application to HMLR to register the transfer of ownership from the seller to the buyer within the 30-working day OS1 priority period

.

MORE BOOKS BY
LAW BRIEF PUBLISHING

A selection of our other titles available now:-

'A Practical Guide to Document Signing and Electronic Signatures for Conveyancers' by Lorraine Richardson
'A Practical Guide to Transgender Law' by Robin Moira White & Nicola Newbegin
'Artificial Intelligence – The Practical Legal Issues (2nd Edition)' by John Buyers
'A Practical Guide to Challenging Sham Marriage Allegations in Immigration Law' by Priya Solanki
'A Practical Guide to New Build Conveyancing' by Paul Sams & Rebecca East
'A Practical Guide to Inherited Wealth on Divorce' by Hayley Trim
'A Practical Guide to Shareholder Disputes in Family Businesses' by Ed Weeks
'A Practical Guide to the Law of Forests in Scotland' by Philip Buchan
'A Practical Guide to Health and Medical Cases in Immigration Law' by Rebecca Chapman & Miranda Butler
'A Practical Guide to Bad Character Evidence for Criminal Practitioners by Aparna Rao
'A Practical Guide to Environmental Enforcement' by Christopher Badger & Stuart Jessop
'A Practical Guide to Hoarding and Mental Health for Housing Lawyers' by Rachel Coyle
'A Practical Guide to Psychiatric Claims in Personal Injury – 2nd Edition' by Liam Ryan
'Stephens on Contractual Indemnities' by Richard Stephens
'A Practical Guide to the EU Succession Regulation' by Richard Frimston
'A Practical Guide to Solicitor and Client Costs – 2nd Edition' by Robin Dunne
'Constructive Dismissal – Practice Pointers and Principles' by Benjimin Burgher

'A Practical Guide to the General Data Protection Regulation (GDPR) – 2nd Edition' by Keith Markham

'Ellis on Credit Hire – Sixth Edition' by Aidan Ellis & Tim Kevan

'A Practical Guide to Working with Litigants in Person and McKenzie Friends in Family Cases' by Stuart Barlow

'Protecting Unregistered Brands: A Practical Guide to the Law of Passing Off' by Lorna Brazell

'A Practical Guide to Secondary Liability and Joint Enterprise Post-Jogee' by Joanne Cecil & James Mehigan

'A Practical Guide to the Pre-Action RTA Claims Protocol for Personal Injury Lawyers' by Antonia Ford

'A Practical Guide to Neighbour Disputes and the Law' by Alexander Walsh

'A Practical Guide to Forfeiture of Leases' by Mark Shelton

'A Practical Guide to Coercive Control for Legal Practitioners and Victims' by Rachel Horman

'A Practical Guide to Rights Over Airspace and Subsoil' by Daniel Gatty

'Tackling Disclosure in the Criminal Courts – A Practitioner's Guide' by Narita Bahra QC & Don Ramble

'A Practical Guide to the Law of Driverless Cars – Second Edition' by Alex Glassbrook, Emma Northey & Scarlett Milligan

'A Practical Guide to TOLATA Claims' by Greg Williams

'A Practical Guide to Elderly Law – 2nd Edition' by Justin Patten

'A Practical Guide to the Law of Prescription in Scotland' by Andrew Foyle

'A Practical Guide to the Construction and Rectification of Wills and Trust Instruments' by Edward Hewitt

'A Practical Guide to the Law of Bullying and Harassment in the Workplace' by Philip Hyland

'How to Be a Freelance Solicitor: A Practical Guide to the SRA-Regulated Freelance Solicitor Model' by Paul Bennett

'A Practical Guide to Prison Injury Claims' by Malcolm Johnson

'A Practical Guide to the Small Claims Track - 2nd Edition' by Dominic Bright

'A Practical Guide to Advising Clients at the Police Station' by Colin Stephen McKeown-Beaumont

'The Law of Houses in Multiple Occupation: A Practical Guide to HMO Proceedings' by Julian Hunt
'Occupiers, Highways and Defective Premises Claims: A Practical Guide Post-Jackson – 2nd Edition' by Andrew Mckie
'A Practical Guide to Financial Ombudsman Service Claims' by Adam Temple & Robert Scrivenor
'A Practical Guide to Advising Schools on Employment Law' by Jonathan Holden
'A Practical Guide to Running Housing Disrepair and Cavity Wall Claims: 2nd Edition' by Andrew Mckie & Ian Skeate
'A Practical Guide to Holiday Sickness Claims – 2nd Edition' by Andrew Mckie & Ian Skeate
'Arguments and Tactics for Personal Injury and Clinical Negligence Claims' by Dorian Williams
'A Practical Guide to Drone Law' by Rufus Ballaster, Andrew Firman, Eleanor Clot
'A Practical Guide to Compliance for Personal Injury Firms Working With Claims Management Companies' by Paul Bennett
'RTA Allegations of Fraud in a Post-Jackson Era: The Handbook – 2nd Edition' by Andrew Mckie
'RTA Personal Injury Claims: A Practical Guide Post-Jackson' by Andrew Mckie
'On Experts: CPR35 for Lawyers and Experts' by David Boyle
'An Introduction to Personal Injury Law' by David Boyle
'A Practical Guide to Subtle Brain Injury Claims' by Pankaj Madan

These books and more are available to order online direct from the publisher at www.lawbriefpublishing.com, where you can also read free sample chapters. For any queries, contact us on 0844 587 2383 or mail@lawbriefpublishing.com.

Our books are also usually in stock at www.amazon.co.uk with free next day delivery for Prime members, and at good legal bookshops such as Wildy & Sons.

We are regularly launching new books in our series of practical day-to-day practitioners' guides. Visit our website and join our free newsletter to be kept informed and to receive special offers, free chapters, etc.

You can also follow us on Twitter at www.twitter.com/lawbriefpub.